Vision

and ITEN History

Compiled by Alison Chant

Vision
and ITEN History

Compiled by Alison Chant

Copyright © 2014 by Vision Publishing

ISBN 978-1-61529-150-2

Vision Publishing
1672 Main Street E 109
Ramona, CA 92065
1 800 9 VISION
www.booksbyvision.com

Table of Contents

The History of
Vision & the ITEN

Introduction

What a year it has been. Since I first became involved with Vision, my personal journey has been rocky at best, and the roller coaster in many ways continues today. Vision International University and ITEN (International Teaching and Education Network) of which I joyfully give leadership, continues to grow, change and mature, and at the same time our challenges continue. Now we are facing challenges of growth, and strategic changes must be made for everyone's vested future.

Each year we have a Vision and Leadership Conference, or what we call our World Zone Leaders conference. We have divided the world into regions, and have developed leaders in each area who are dedicated to seeing the *Whole Word taken to the Whole World*. This is the motto of ITEN/Vision since its inception in 1974. In 2007, we met in Athens, Greece, with our Mediterranean and European World Zone leadership, and leaders from around the world.

After a time of fellowship and renewing friendships, we settled into our meetings on the World Zone system and accreditation. Who would have thought that we would have such an extensive outreach, with such quality leaders from around the world?

From Eastern Europe, Dr. Ernie Campe and his wife Linda reported that the Vision schools are growing in their region.

As of today, they are working with over 1500 students in five nations and working with fifty-five local churches.

In the Middle East, Dr. Jerry Zandstra and Yvette D'Sousa, along with Dr. Tim and Laurie Dailey report that the outreach is making a real impact. In partnership with the International School of Ministry, hundreds of students are being trained, and we are expanding into Jordan and other Middle Eastern nations.

In Western Europe we have added five new schools. Those are in Switzerland, Italy and the UK. Denis Plant is heading to the UK in May to solidify arrangements for more schools in England, which is a real answer to prayer.

Africa continues to grow, under Dr. Steve Mills, our recipient of the annual Excellence in Leadership Award, and we are getting ready for greater launches in India and China, along with Farsi language programs in partnership with the Iranian Christian Church.

Overall our meetings were highly productive, a true blessing to all who could attend.

In the Steps of Paul

The second half of our time in Greece was a tour, following the Footsteps of Paul. At each stop, we heard dynamic teaching from Dr. Chant, Dr. Gurley, Dr. West, Dr. Zandstra, and Dr. Brian van Deventer and Dr. Gail Stathis. Drs. Brian and Gail, along with their staff in Greece, made this a most memorable time for all.

Reflections

When I wrote this, I was still in Greece, teaching 20+ students about leadership. Our staff was home preparing for our Readiness Visit (February 28) from the Distance Education and Training Council, the next step in our march towards accreditation. As always, I am grateful to the Lord for the privilege of serving in this ministry. God is so good and merciful. We have much work to complete before we can move to the next level in Excellence, but the Lord is our helper, and we will indeed make it by His grace. We must always stay focused on taking *the Whole Word to the Whole World,* as God gives us strength. One key to doing this is to never forget where we have come from. The reason for this book is to document the first 30 plus years of a remarkable and unlikely work for the Lord; the Vision International University/ITEN story begins here.

Dr. Stan DeKoven
President

Chapter One

The Athens Conference

Report of the 2007 Vision Conference by Ken Chant, our Australian Founder of Vision.

From our house in Sydney, Australia to the Fenix Hotel in Athens, Greece took 35 hours of travel. We arrived exhausted, but we propped our eyes open, for we could not possibly miss the first session of the Vision World Zone Leaders Conference. A fine message was presented by Dr Stan Dekoven, the international president of the college. He spoke on the future of Vision and inspired us all. The next day (Tuesday) was wholly occupied with conference meetings, reports, strategy discussions, and the like. We were informed that currently the college has around 125,000 students in 143 countries. Also our African graduates have planted more than 1000 churches in West Africa during the past year with an average size of 75 people.

The actual conference ended at noon on Wednesday, whereupon all those who had chosen to remain in Greece for the tour, "In the Missionary Steps of the Apostle Paul," boarded the 50-seat bus, filling every seat, and we set off for Thessaloniki, some 600 km north. This modern city (the second largest in Greece) has the same name and spelling (in Greek) as the biblical one. Then, after I had given a 30-minute talk to the group, based on a passage from Paul's letter to the Thessalonians, we visited a museum, toured the city, and travelled about 100 kms to Kavala. This town is the port of ancient Philippi, and the place where the apostle Paul first set foot on European soil. Philippi itself is some distance inland, and extensive and impressive ruins of the city can be seen, including the probable place where Paul and Silas were imprisoned after they had been illegally flogged. They were released from their chains by an earthquake, and praising God for their miraculous deliverance left Philippi, having established the first Christian church in Europe.

We found it rather awe-inspiring to look at stones, and walk on pathways, that the apostle himself once saw and trod.

Greece, like Australia, is suffering from a severe drought, so the mountainous countryside is dry and brown, and the rivers low, with only an occasional patch of green in an otherwise parched landscape. But the drive from Athens to Thessaloniki, then on to Kavala and Philippi was nonetheless spectacular, with every corner bringing a new vista of mountains and valleys, rivers and lakes, and the beautiful coastline. The bus was rather cramped, and not overly-comfortable, but the things we saw along the way and at each stopping point made it all more than worthwhile.

On Friday we returned to Athens, arriving at about 2200 hours for a very late dinner. On that return trip we finally saw Mount Olympus, which we missed on the way north, because night had fallen. However, we had no time to stop and had to content ourselves with a view from the highway, a few kilometres distance from the mountain. On the way south we also detoured to Berea (now called Verria), where Paul found a welcome after he had been obliged to flee from Thessalonica by night. Standing in front of a monument to Paul, I gave a 15-minute talk on the mystery of the "nobility" of the Berean Jews (in contrast with the attitude of the Jews in Thessalonica).

Saturday took us to the Peloponnese, the site of much dramatic ancient history. We crossed the impressive Corinthian Canal (which has turned the Peloponnese into an Island), and drove to the site of the ruins of ancient Corinth.

These too are quite extensive, and very impressive, complete with a museum containing a fine array of ancient sculptures. We also visited briefly the mountain-top site of an old and massive Crusader fortress that stands high above the ruins. A picture of it, along with a brief description, can be seen by looking up "Acrocorinth" in Wikipedia (http://en.wikipedia. org/wiki/Acrocorinth).

In Corinth, among the ruins, I gave another 30-minute talk, based on Paul's statement to the Corinthians. *"When I came to you brothers, I did not come to you with eloquence or superior wisdom as I proclaimed to you the testimony about God. For I resolved to know nothing while I was with you, except Jesus Christ and him crucified. I came to you in weakness and fear, and with much trembling"* (1 Corinthians 2:1-3). After my talk Brian Deventer, the Director of the European and Middle Eastern Mission, who hosted our trip through Greece, pointed out a stone at our feet with the name of a New Testament character clearly gouged into the stone. We could not believe it was just lying there exposed to the elements. Erastus is mentioned by Paul in Romans 16:23; *"Erastus, who is the city's director of public works, and our brother Quartius send you greetings."* The fact that Erastus was the director of public works explained why the sign was there.

There also, on an elevated spot overlooking the ruins, I conducted the wedding service for a young American couple, David and Shannon Richardson, who had decided to postpone their wedding until it could be performed in Greece.

Today (Sunday afternoon) we visited the Acropolis, but heavy rain forced us to abandon our tour half-way through. I took a few photos, but the grey day will have washed all colour out of them. Happily we will be here for another two weeks, and hopefully we will be given at least one bright sunny day that will enable us to try again.

This is February 2007. There were 55 delegates at the Vision Conference. Who were these delegates? What is Vision Bible College? How did it all begin? How did it evolve into Vision International University? For that, we must start at the beginning.

Ken Chant

Chapter Two

The Providence of God

Stories gathered from the Chant family.

God works in mysterious ways to bring about his purposes. If James Chant had not caught polio at the age of six, he would have become a farmer like his brothers, and his sons would probably have been content to follow him into farming. As it was, because of the polio, James developed a weakness in his legs which meant farming was impossible for him, so he was sent to the city to be educated. In time, he became a teacher, and therefore his children had increased opportunity for study and advancement, which could otherwise have been denied them. As it is, both sons became pastors and great Bible teachers. Ken established Vision College, which has spread to more than 140 countries, while Barry established Tabor Bible College, which has campuses in several Australian states and students throughout Australasia and Indonesia.

Ken's early years.

Kenneth David (1933-) was the first born son of James and Vera Chant, and he showed a precocious bent from his earliest years, reading, for example, through the ten large volumes of a children's encyclopedia by the time he was ten years of age. Indeed, he never lost a thirst for knowledge and throughout his life has maintained an interest in many fields, such as science, astronomy, music and history. After accepting the Lord as his Saviour, theology became his first love and continues to fascinate him; although he has been studying it for over fifty years.

In his own words, *"I cannot remember a moment of my life when I was not aware of God. From my earliest years He has always been very real to me, although I did not know him as Saviour until my ninth year."*

During his childhood, Ken suffered a speech impediment, which caused him much embarrassment. His problem was that he would open his mouth to say a word and find he was incapable of uttering that word. Because of this, he compensated by learning similes so that he could quickly substitute for the word he was striving to pronounce. This became the foundation of the enormous vocabulary which helped in his preaching in later years. If he could not say one word then he had two or three others at hand to continue speaking. Unfortunately, this did not work when he was asked to read aloud in school so he suffered misunderstandings and much humiliation from his fellow students.

Many times during his childhood, Ken's life was at risk, but the Lord had a work planned for him and so his life was continually preserved. Around the age of seven, he was at a lonely beach with his mother and his sister and brother when he was caught in a riptide while swimming in the sea. He was convinced he was about to drown when suddenly a man appeared out of nowhere and rescued him, taking him back to the shore. Ken ran to tell his mother what had happened. When he reached her, he turned to show her who had rescued him but the man had disappeared! There was no way the man could have gone from that vast beach so quickly. Because of this, Ken has always been convinced that the man must have been an angel sent by God to rescue him and so preserve his life.

In 1941 during World War Two, when Ken was eight years of age, he was involved in an accident. His father had to stop his car suddenly on the way to see the troopship, "The Queen Elizabeth." In those days, there were no seat belts so Ken went through the windscreen and the glass sliced a huge scar across his face from his left eye across his nose and down his right cheek. This disfigurement also caused him great mental and emotional anguish and resulted in him becoming even more withdrawn. This caused Ken to develop a certain diffidence in dealing with others. Fortunately, he had a sister and brother by this time, and the rough and tumble of daily family living went a long way toward helping Ken to grow into a balanced and healthy boy. Certainly, when later on he began his public ministry and stepped behind the pulpit to speak for God, he became absolutely fearless in his preaching.

Commander Harvey

Around nine years of age Ken accepted the Lord as his Saviour and this came about in an unusual way. Commander Harvey, a Christian man, determined he would speak about Christ to as many children as he could during his retirement. To catch their attention, he bought a gypsy caravan, which he painted bright colors and decorated with memorabilia of his years at sea. He had been the captain of a windjammer in the days of the wind-driven Merchant Navy, where he learned to reverence the God of the deep.

"Others went out on the sea in ships; they were merchants on the mighty waters. They saw the works of the Lord, his wonderful deeds in the deep. For he spoke and stirred up a tempest that lifted high the waves. They mounted up to the heavens and went down to the depths; in their peril their courage melted away." (Psalm 107:23-26).

Commander Harvey would drive his gypsy caravan up to the school gateway and park it right outside. When classes had ended and children were coming out, they saw the caravan and gathered around him. There he kept them enthralled with his stories, bringing into his life experiences the gospel of Jesus and the salvation he promises to all, even children.

Ken remembers him as a grizzled old seaman, with a massive beard and a big brass ship's bell, which he rang to gain the attention of the children. He spoke with a hoarse voice developed from his years of roaring over Atlantic gales and waved his massive cutlass in the air as he told many great stories about his days at sea.

To determine who had accepted the Lord, he instructed the school children to write out their testimony and give it to him. He promised that whoever did this would receive a New Testament. This Ken did; it was his first spiritual experience and was to culminate in a life committed totally to God.

During the years that followed, Ken's mother, Vera, made sure the children attended Sunday school at the Finsbury Park Baptist Church, South Australia. She herself played the piano for some of the meetings and took a lively interest in her children's spiritual development. In family life, Ken's father was a strict disciplinarian; he believed that to spare the rod was to spoil the child. Ken must have been a mischievous child as he can remember many a miserable hour waiting in the bathroom for his father to arrive with the leather strap. He thought at the time it was refined torture on his father's part, but in hindsight, he realizes his father was waiting for his temper to cool.

High School years

During his high school years, it became apparent that Ken was developing a writing skill, which was to help him in years to come. He became editor of three Woodville District High School Term papers, and during his intermediate year, he was editor of the *Woodville High School Magazine*. He has happy memories of his time there. However, a great sadness was to enter the family in Ken's fifteenth year, and for a time this was to cause a disruption in his development.

This was the death of his dear and much loved mother, from cancer, at the early age of thirty-eight. At the time of her illness, she also gave birth to a little girl, Christine, who died almost immediately after she was born, so the family had a double tragedy, which affected their lives for years to come.

This tragedy occurred before the days of counseling, so the family had to bear their pain, each in his or her own way, but there is no doubt that it deeply affected all of them. Ken's father never remarried but remained a widower until he died at the age of ninety-four.

Ken gives himself to God for fulltime service.

On Easter Saturday 1949, two months before his sixteenth birthday, Ken was attending a Baptist Youth Camp, at Clare in South Australia. That night the preacher challenged the young people to get serious with God. He did not call them to the front but told them to find a quiet place out under the stars to ask God what he required of them. Ken found a place under a huge and ancient gum tree and wrestled in prayer for some hours. He knew God was calling him for full time service, but he had his own ambition, to become a millionaire by the time he was forty. Finally, he gave in to God and dedicated himself to full time service.

Unknown to him, on that same Easter Saturday, his future wife Alison, almost fifteen, was being baptized in the Holy Spirit and determining that she too would give her life to God for full time service. They did not meet for another three and a half years, when Ken himself received the baptism in the Holy Spirit.

Alison's early years.

Alison was the fourth child of five born to James and Laurel McIntyre. Her father went away to war when she was five and returned when she was eleven. The family only saw him once on leave from Tobruk during the six years he was away.

He came home weighing only seven stone, which was not much for a six foot man. After that leave he went back to fight in New Guinea and finally came home with a dose of Malaria which plagued him for many years.

The family was in strained financial circumstances, and Laurel helped by making and mending clothes with her Singer sewing machine, and hammering extra soles onto boots and shoes using a shoe last. She taught her children their prayers and sent them to Sunday school, though she did not often get to church herself. For many years Laurel's mother, Grandma Wright, lived with the family. Alison can remember walking Grandma to church on a Sunday evening.

Grandma Wright was a deeply religious woman and she felt privileged to hear Smith Wigglesworth when he came to Australia. Alison remembers her Grandma praying for her and laying hands on her to bless her when she was nearing the age of thirteen.

From her earliest years Alison wondered how she could become a Christian and prayed that God would send someone to explain this to her. In her twelfth year her prayers was answered. Her older brother James accepted the Lord as his Saviour and came home to witness to his family. Alison and her sister Barbara accepted immediately and were baptized in water at the Colonel Light Gardens Church of Christ. Later when James received the baptism in the Holy Spirit Alison too was filled, and she and James both joined the Christian Revival Crusade. James later became a pastor for the Assembly of God churches.

The Christian Revival Crusade, which is now called CRC Churches International, is a Pentecostal church, which began in Australia under the leadership of Leo Harris and Tom Foster just after the Second World War. When James and Alison joined, it was still a very young church with only two or three congregations; now it has some 800 churches in Australia and overseas locations as well.

Alison attended the Edwardstown Primary School where she too encountered Commander Harvey when he visited her school. Later she attended the Adelaide Girls High School where she gained her Intermediate Certificate in 1950.

She had a serious illness during her fourteenth year and was in danger of losing her life, but after a life saving operation she recovered completely. This meant she missed 6 months of school, which necessitated an extra year to gain her Intermediate Certificate. After leaving school she worked at the Government Post Office for a year and then went on to begin a nursing career at the Royal Adelaide Hospital.

Ken could not settle into a job after leaving high school, so his father sent him into the country to work for his Uncle Bob who had a farm near Mt. Gambier. The hard work developed Ken's physique, for he learned to ride horses, milk cows, herd sheep, dig post holes, string wire fences, and all the other tasks of a busy mixed farm. His uncle became ill because of his years as a prisoner of war, and for a time could not do any outside work. Ken took over the farm attending to countless chores.

While working for his uncle, Ken experienced two more instances of the providence of God. The first was when he and his uncle were attempting to erect a windmill. As they raised the heavy structure, the wind caught it and it began to fall. Had it fallen straight it would have killed Ken, who was right in its path, but quick as a flash, his uncle sprang forward and deflected the windmill to the side, causing it to miss Ken by inches. It is known that in an emergency a man can be given superhuman strength and this certainly seems to have been the case with Uncle Bob as the windmill was extremely heavy and there is no way he could have pushed it aside normally.

In January 1950, Ken became violently ill and because his uncle's farm was some distance from Mt Gambier Ken diagnosed himself with the help of a medical book. He had a swollen appendix so his uncle took him in the back of a truck over the rough country roads to the Mount Gambier hospital some 25 miles away. When they arrived and Ken was examined the doctors were amazed that, considering the bumpy ride, his appendix had not ruptured. As it was, they operated just in time, for back in 1950; a ruptured appendix could mean certain death. Unfortunately, there were further complications and some days later, another operation had to be performed to relieve a strangulated bowel caused by the first operation. After Ken had recovered from these two operations, his father took him home to Adelaide but his troubles were not over. Ken became ill yet again, and this time his father took him in to the Royal Adelaide Hospital. The doctors there did not think his condition serious and were all for sending him home again but his father refused and insisted on leaving him in hospital overnight. This decision saved Ken's life as he was operated on that night for yet another strangulated bowel. Had his father taken him home as requested there is no way he could have returned him to the hospital in time, and Ken would have died in agony.

All of these operations left Ken weak, and it took some time for him to get his strength back. There was no thought of returning to the farm, and Ken eventually started work in Adelaide.

As he regained his strength, he threw himself into the Lord's work. He became a very enthusiastic Baptist and was appointed State Secretary of Christian Endeavour and State Secretary of the Home Missions department in South Australia. Eventually he began to preach in two Baptist churches and became assistant pastor at Seaton Park and Prospect churches.

Ken's brother Barry's memories of Ken

Partly because of his speech impediment Ken was a loner, and I can remember once on a Sunday school picnic, Ken sat in a carriage by himself while all of the other children were in the next carriage together.

Ken was always busy; there were so many things he wanted to do and so much to explore. One of his hobbies was building a crystal set and then later a radio. He used to play LPs of piano music at night, before he drifted off to sleep. He had a large collection of jazz and classical piano music. He also took art classes, learned lettering, dabbled in weaving, and other crafts, and learned to play the banjo mandolin.

He loved boogie-woogie music and taught himself to play it on the piano. He used to shut the dining room door and play for hours at night.

He was relatively disinterested in sports, although if he did go to a football match he would cheer and shout passionately with the best of them.

How Ken received the Baptism in the Holy Spirit

In 1951, at the age of eighteen, Ken became friendly with a brother and sister, Lyall and Bonnie Phillips, who witnessed to him about the baptism in the Holy Spirit. At first, he refused to believe it could be true, but he went along to the Adelaide Circulating Library and studied all the books he could find with arguments against the experience.

In his own words, *"The arguments against the Baptism were so insubstantial I was convinced that the Baptism was indeed for today."*

He went along to the then Christian Revival Crusade church in Sturt Street, Adelaide, and eventually received this wonderful experience and spoke in tongues for some two to three hours at a prayer meeting in the home of Vic and Cicely Schroeder.

At that time the Baptist Union was antagonistic to the baptism in the Holy Spirit so, as Barry has indicated above, Ken was asked to leave and his career in the Baptist church came to an abrupt end. He transferred to the CRC where he had received the Baptism.

Once he received the baptism in the Holy Spirit, he was so fired up by this experience he was like an Old Testament prophet. He was due to give his testimony at an open-air Baptist Youth Rally, I think at Waterfall Gully, in November 1952, and when he did, it was all about his experience in the Spirit. It caused a reaction. His friend David White, who became a Baptist minister and was years later himself baptized in the Spirit, protested that it was 'not doctrinal.' Ken snorted with disgust -- for him the Bible came before any doctrine. At that time, Ken was planning to go into the Baptist College training for the ministry. He was preaching monthly at both Prospect and Seaton Baptist churches in South Australia. He preached one night at Prospect on being baptized in the Spirit. I understand that a day or so later, he received a phone call telling him his speaking services were no longer required. He was appalled that the Baptist authorities did not even call him in to speak with him.

A few weeks before this, Ken was advocating that our Baptist church put on Saturday dances to attract young people. After his experience in the Spirit, he stood up in a meeting and passionately urged the church to start prayer meetings instead!

Ken was a big help to me. It was through him praying for me that I was filled with the Holy Spirit; a story that is told in a couple of my books. Ken advised me on the best books to read. I remember one night shortly after being baptized in the Holy Spirit; I was going to the pictures with some young people from church. He just said that since being filled with the Holy Spirit, he couldn't do that. So I didn't go. At times when I was struggling with personal issues, I sought his wisdom. When he lived in Woomera for a time, I used to write to him. After he was married and living in Ballarat this continued from time to time. Later, in 1963, it was Ken who persuaded me to leave Murray Bridge and join the staff at Sturt Street CRC. "What if I take your advice and it proves to be wrong?" I asked. "That's your stupid fault for taking my advice," he answered, with his usual care and compassion.

At the CRC church, led by Leo Harris, Ken met Alison and they began to go out together. After nine months, Ken and Alison became engaged on May 23rd 1953.

At this crucial time, while Ken was doing his National Service Training for the Australian Army, he decided to become a conscientious objector. He refused to attend any more weekends of training. This could have meant a jail sentence but he was determined to go ahead. Fortunately, he had a very friendly Captain who tried very hard to keep Ken from being arrested by the Military Police. But then Ken moved to Ballarat to pastor a small church, and at once, as a pastor, became exempt from compulsory military service, so all was well.

Prior to that, Ken worked for a short time at the Woomera Rocket Range and then moved to Melbourne to begin training for the Pentecostal ministry. He decided to pursue this training in Melbourne CRC under Pastor Lloyd Longfield, so he and Alison were parted for the whole of the nine months they were engaged except for two or three weekends. This too was training for the future when Alison would be left with their children from time to time while Ken held various crusades around Australia. They wrote many letters to each other during those nine months.

After a year and a half of nursing training, Alison became very ill with a toxic thyroid and required another operation. This put an end to her career as a nurse and after her recovery; she and Ken were married on the 6th March 1954 at the Goodwood Baptist church by Pastor Leo Harris. Ken and Alison had been through deep waters, but the testing times were not over.

Chapter Three

Our First Faith Adventures

With much updated material added the following pages are written by Alison and they come from the book, *"Discovery"*

We learn our first lessons! (1954-1955)

"Well, Ken and Alison, Ballarat needs a pastor; how would you like to go there?"

Our senior pastor paused to see what effect his words would have on us. Eagerly we nodded our heads.

"Of course! We're ready whenever you are. We'll go*!*"

We didn't have to pray about it, because for many months we had been asking God for an open door. The need was there, we had been looking for a place to go to; we were ready. It was as simple as that! So for three months we remained in our jobs and travelled by train seventy-five miles every weekend from Melbourne to Ballarat. After those twelve weeks, the congregation invited Ken to be their pastor, and we moved into an apartment on Main St.

Ken had studied hard to become an effective pastor, but there were still many things that could only be taught by God. True men of God are tutored by the Holy Spirit!

Our first year flew by. Ken took a job in a large department store, selling men's clothing to take care of our physical needs. Our eldest son, Dale, was born; Ken took his first funeral; some of our congregation moved away; others came to fill their place. By the end of the year, we had gained seven members - and lost seven! We still had the grand total of twenty-one members! Did we feel we had missed God's guidance? No! We were full of enthusiasm and zeal, praising God, sure that a remarkable breakthrough was coming.

In the second year, God honoured our confidence. Prayer was offered for the wife of the editor of our local newspaper, and she received an amazing healing from heart trouble. She proved to be a born evangelist, and our church began to grow.

Our first faith venture

We walked one day through a local park, enjoying the warmth of a delightful summer day and the breeze dancing among the leaves of the trees. One of our favourite places was an old-fashioned glasshouse filled with exotic begonias and marvellous statuary. We arrived there and sat on the lawn beside it, soaking up the sunshine, watching our eager little son chase the birds.

We had come there because we had a problem to discuss and to pray about. Ken was finding it increasingly difficult to fulfil all his duties as a pastor while having to rely upon public transport, or his own feet! We were wondering about the possibility of buying a car - or perhaps I should say more accurately, we were asking ourselves how we could possibly find the money to buy a car! Ken's wages did not permit such an extravagance. But perhaps we could "step out in faith" and trust God to meet the cost?

If only we could have looked into the future! This was going to be an opportunity for us to learn a vital lesson in faith and guidance. We were about to enter blindly the realm of presumption. Like Abraham of old, we would be taught the importance of doing things God's way.

Only we didn't know that then!

"There's no doubt about it, we do need a car," I said. "It's getting difficult to visit people by bus or by walking, especially when you have to continue your work at the department store."

"Very well, we've established the need, let's pray about it and believe God for a car," said Ken decisively.

"We don't have enough money to make payments each month," I reasoned. "There's the rent, food, and clothing bills. We have a child to support now, I don't see how we can manage the extra expense."

"Just believe, Honey, that's all we have to do. We'll make the down payment, and then believe God to bring in the needed funds each month."

"Right," I agreed.

It would be such a relief to have a car, especially with the baby. Surely God didn't want us to have to walk the streets at night, wheeling our baby to meetings in the cold night air of the coming autumn? Surely he would honour our faith and somehow provide the extra money we needed?

Yes, God did want us to have a car; he even had one picked out for us, which someone would freely give us. But we didn't know that then. So we rushed in ahead of God and chose our own vehicle! It became an expensive lesson, another example of what happens when (like Abraham) a servant of God becomes impatient and tries to force the Father's hand. Instead of "Isaac" (the child of promise), "Ishmael" is born, with sorrowful consequences.

We made the down payment, and then sat back and waited for God to increase our income by the needed amount each month. It didn't happen!

We couldn't believe it!

Slowly and painfully we came to the realisation that we had gone ahead of God. This was not his way. We could not dictate to him, nor tell him how to achieve his goals, nor how to answer our prayers.

We had to face the humiliation of returning the car to the dealer, and explaining to him that we couldn't make the payments. Of course we lost our deposit, which was considerable. Then we had to confess to our church and our friends what had happened.

A few weeks later, a friend who was a pastor purchased a new car, and then asked us if we would like his old one. So we had our car free of charge! It was in this little Hillman car, not very much later, that God was going to teach us another lesson about his guidance and protection.

Saved by angels! (1956)

How marvellous it was to have a vehicle at last! We thanked God from our hearts for the Father's kind provision. Our lesson learned, we threw ourselves with renewed vigour into the work of the church. By winter we were ready for a vacation. We decided to visit our parents in Adelaide, 400 miles away.

We drove out of Ballarat along a magnificent memorial avenue of trees, planted by the relatives of soldiers killed during the war. Our conversation as we began the journey was again about the puzzling aspects of divine guidance.

"Ken, how can we be sure that we are in the will of God? How can we know that this trip is his will? Does he expect us to ask him about every little thing, or should we just live our lives normally, and only ask his guidance for specific things?"

"I asked an older pastor about that very thing recently," Ken began, *"and he gave me an answer I'll never forget. It's like this. You should first pray and ask for God's guidance,*

and then simply believe that he has heard your prayer. After that, it becomes God's task to make sure you are in his will."

"But what if you aren't in his will," I queried.

"Then he will manoeuvre circumstances until you are in his will. Don't you see? So long as you trust God, the obligation is no longer yours, but his."

Slowly I began to relax as we sped through the vast Australian countryside. I thanked God for another lesson learned. It was so simple. A concept that would stand us in good stead in the years to come. No more agonising over whether we were in the will of God, just a simple prayer of faith -

"Father, we want to be in the centre of your will. So from now on, we will simply trust that we are there. We know that you will then honour our faith and arrange circumstances to ensure that we do not deviate from your path for us. Amen."

I cuddled my little son in my arms and drifted off to sleep, (This was in the days before seat belts were invented) secure in the knowledge that God himself was watching over us. He was in control of our lives and he would guide and direct us, shaping at least the outcome of each event, if not the event itself.

I didn't know it then, but it would not be very long before we would have a terrifying opportunity to experience this very protection.

A few days after arriving in Adelaide and sharing a joyful reunion with our families, we decided to take a trip to Victor Harbour. This is a beautiful part of the South Australian shoreline, and a popular picnic spot.

We expected a time of refreshing in body and spirit.

The air was chilly, but the sky was blue, the sun was brightly shining, and it was a perfect day for a country drive. So we motored through the hills, revelling in the glorious views stretched out before us.

The time together at the beach was everything we had hoped for, and when we finally packed up to return home we were weary but rejuvenated. It had been delightful to play with our baby son on the beautiful white sands, and to paddle with him in the salt water.

As we travelled through the twisting winding hills on our return journey we noticed a sign on the side of the road, "STEEP INCLINE" Naturally, we expected to find a sharply rising hill after the next turn in the road. So Ken accelerated to accommodate the slope. Alas, instead of an upgrade we found to our horror that we were plunging down a steep decline (not an incline). Our car only had mechanical brakes, and when the drums were hot after a long trip, as they were now, they did not function very well.

It all happened so quickly. Afterward Ken told me he was sure we were going to die. He remembers distinctly crying out, *"Lord, here we come!"*

We were travelling too fast. We were gaining speed. The brakes were ineffective, and we could not make the next corner. Instead, we would be hurtled into space to smash onto the valley floor far below.

But God had not finished with us yet! He had other plans for us. Just as the car was about to go over the edge it stopped! Just like that! We sat there, shaken but alive, praising God for deliverance from a terrible death.

There was absolutely no natural reason why our car should have halted on the edge of that cliff. We could only suppose God had intervened in that moment - perhaps by an angel - to arrest the vehicle. There was no slowing down. One moment we were travelling at high speed, and the next we had come to an abrupt halt - yet we were not jolted, nor hurt in the slightest.

We backed up slowly and then, with trembling but thankful hearts, travelled the remainder of our way home. How grateful we were to the Lord for this sign that we were indeed in his will and under his protection!

A week later, we were to experience yet another instance of God's tender care.

We were travelling back to Ballarat through the Adelaide Hills, and looking forward to another year of fruitful work for the Lord. Suddenly we saw a car wheel roll past us on the left. It trundled to a stop and leaned crazily against the fence on the side of the road.

Meanwhile our car lurched, and we realised with a shock that we had been watching one of our own back wheels! Ken quickly stopped the car and we tumbled out to assess the damage.

"Thank God it was the back wheel," Ken exclaimed. *"Had it been a front wheel we could have been killed or been the cause of a terrible accident."*

We were so young and inexperienced! Did we have any tools, or even a jack? We began to look.

Just then, two policemen in a car pulled up beside us. They had seen the whole thing and had stopped to help us.

"Do you have any tools?" they asked.

With some embarrassment, Ken had to reply, *"Well, you see officer, this is our first car, and we aren't very well equipped yet."*

"Let me help," laughed the policeman. He got out his wheel jack and tools, and in no time had our wheel back on. Then

he gave us a lesson in mechanics. He tightened the nuts on all the other wheels, while patiently explaining that it is a good idea, before starting on a long journey, to check your wheels - especially on a car built in 1938!

Feeling a little foolish, we thanked the two officers heartily, and continued on our way. We praised God that a rear wheel, and not one of our front ones, had come off first. We thanked God also for an understanding policeman with a sense of humour.

"I wonder, did you arrange to have him ride behind us Lord, or was it just a coincidence?"

Chapter Four

Alison Continues Her story.

Sorrow Turned To Joy! (1955-1960)

When God wants to drill a man
And thrill a man
And skill a man
When God wants to mold a man
To play the noblest part;
When He yearns with all His heart
To create so great and bold a man
That all the world shall be amazed
Watch His methods, watch His ways!
How He ruthlessly perfects
Whom He royally elects!
How He hammers him and hurts him
And with mighty blows converts him
Into trial shapes of clay which
Only God understands;
While his tortured heart is crying
And he lifts beseeching hands!
How He bends but never breaks
When his good He undertakes;
How He uses whom He chooses
And with every purpose fuses him;
By every act induces him,
to try His splendour out...
God knows what He's about.
(J Oswald Sanders; Spiritual Leadership; pg.141)

Something was seriously wrong! Ken and I had always wanted a large family. During our courtship we had joked about having twelve children after our marriage, and had both eagerly looked forward to lots of babies.

We had one dear little son, but he was growing older and we wanted to give him a brother or sister to enjoy.

Tragedy struck! I became pregnant only to lose the baby at two months. Later I became pregnant again only to lose yet another child.

As I look back over the years, I can recognise the deep work done within us by these happenings. But then I could not see the coming heartbreak, nor the overwhelming joy of God's final triumph over all our despair. I know why God will not let us look too far ahead: we could not bear the knowledge!

I can also see how the Father uses tragedy to build character, compassion, and toughness of spirit into his people. His goal is to refine and mould them into strong men and women of God.

He does not personally send illness or accident. These are just part of life. But he does use them. Nothing is wasted. The Lord weaves every thread of experience into the fabric of our personality as we learn to yield ourselves to him and to rely on him totally.

My doctor discovered I had some small fibroid tumours and he wanted to operate, but I refused. I preferred to believe God for my healing and began to fast and pray.

God has healed my body and met our physical needs often, each in a new and different way.

I felt wonderful after my fast, and had boundless energy. Scriptures filled my mind; I allowed no negative thoughts to enter. Life was good. Nine months later, I learned that God had answered prayer, and that the tumours had disappeared.

But by then it didn't seem to matter very much. A new sorrow had fallen upon us, casting a bleak shadow over our happiness. Our home would never be the same again.

Gavin is born and dies (1957-1961)

We had left our first church in Ballarat Victoria and moved to a young church in Springvale, a hundred miles away. There, on the second of November, I gave birth by caesarian section to a dear little four-and-a-half pound baby boy. He was with us just two days. On the fourth of November, he went to be with Jesus. Heaven will always seem very near to us because one of our little ones is there waiting for us. We named him Gavin James and laid him to rest in the Necropolis cemetery at Spring Vale.

Little Gavin's life was so brief because of a condition called placentia praevia. I had lost part of the placenta at six months and then he had been born by caesarian section at seven and a half months. He was terribly bruised, and died two days later.

We were devastated. As I lay there in hospital, all I could say was *"Why, Lord, why did you allow this to happen to us?"*

Ken tried to comfort me.

"I don't know why, but I do know this," he said, *"one day God will explain everything."*

Clinging to this thought brought comfort to me over the next painful weeks and months.

"God, my little one will never know the joys of this life. He will never be able to play ball, or eat chocolate, or gambol in the waves of the sea. He will never laugh and play with his older brother."

"Neither will he have to experience any sorrow," was the gentle reply.

Each time I closed my eyes I was given a picture of Jesus holding my little baby close in his arms. He seemed to say that baby Gavin was safe with him; and with that, I must be content.

One day, lying on my hospital bed, I watched two little sparrows flirting, their tails bobbing, and twittering happily, as they gathered material for their nest.

"Life goes on," I thought. *"How good God is to give me this message through two of his smallest and humblest creatures."*

Sharon is born.

If Ken and I could have seen into the future during those dark days, we would have been consoled. God would recompense us for the suffering we were going through. He was to grant us not only a darling daughter, but two more precious sons to give us much happiness.

Before then, however, we had to work through a great test of our faith and to gain an enormous victory for the Lord. It would be a vindication of God's healing power, which he would allow us to take around the world. Through this testimony, many other couples, yearning for children, would find faith to have their prayers answered by God.

That story will be told later on in this history, but meanwhile I needed a period of healing and recuperation. The doctor assured me I had no tumours. The reason for my miscarriages was still a mystery to him.

During the following year, I built up my strength. We also moved to Adelaide, where Ken was asked to become an assistant pastor in our home church, under Pastor Leo Harris.

Finally, when Dale was five and a half years of age, we were able to place in his arms a little sister, Sharon Elizabeth Rae.

To bear her I had to remain bedfast for seven months (from when I was six weeks pregnant until she was born at eight and a half months). Many times, it seemed we would lose her, but always God intervened, and at last, she was born safely.

The mystery of my miscarriages was also revealed by the specialist. I had RH-negative blood and had built up antibodies against my babies. Sharon had to have her blood exchanged when she was two days of age. After that, all was well. We were happy and contented. Our little family was growing.

Extraordinary guidance!

My pregnancy with Sharon occurred during a difficult time in Ken's ministry. Pastor Leo Harris, our senior pastor, had many invitations to preach all over the USA. He decided to accept them, and with his wife Belle and their daughter Cherith, a set the date for their departure.

We disclosed the news of my pregnancy, which was already proving to be a difficult one, but after some discussion, we all decided that Leo and Belle should go ahead with their plans. We agreed to trust the Lord for my baby to be born normally. Knowing that they were praying earnestly for us, and that everywhere they ministered in the USA others would also seek the Lord on our behalf, was a great comfort to me as the trying months progressed.

The church, about 500 strong, was left in Ken's hands. He was 27 years old. Added to the church there was a Bible college, a widely circulated magazine, and a nation-wide radio network. Even with a strong team of dedicated men to help him, it was a daunting task.

Half-way through the year, when the Harris family had been gone about 6 months, Ken began to undergo a severe trial.

He felt he could not burden me with it because of my pregnancy, so he battled it alone.

The test was this: his faith gave way, and he no longer believed in anything! Nothing had any meaning for him. He could not feel a particle of assurance! He reached out for God, and could not touch him! The sky was like brass above him and the earth as iron beneath his feet. Yet he continued preaching, praying for the people, teaching in the Bible college, publishing the magazine, speaking on radio, and running the church.

He knew instinctively that if he continued to do the work he'd been called to do that eventually he would come through and regain his faith. So despite the dark shadow that was on his spirit, he persevered in prayer and ministry.

I found an interesting verse, which explains this experience and could help other pastors who may go through a similar experience. It is in the Life of King Hezekiah in 2 Chronicles 33b. *"God left him to test him and to know everything that was in his heart."* This idea of God's testing times is repeated in Deuteronomy 8:2.

For three months, he suffered, until finally, God lifted the veil and he could see again with the eye of faith. Now followed a series of miracles that were many and diverse in nature: blind and deaf people were cured through prayer; some people with cancer were made whole; other illnesses were overcome, and we had the ongoing miracle of the baby in my womb being preserved month after month, despite the complication of my RH-negative blood!

Ken had not prayed for this breakthrough; it came unsought because he stuck steadfastly to the principle of believing that he was in the centre of God's will. The Father then had to get him there and keep him there!

When the Harris family returned, we were able to share with them the great things the Lord had done. We were glad to hand back to them a church that had grown in numbers, and we rejoiced together in our God, who is always there, and who does all things well.

Chapter Five

We Move to Tasmania (1963-1978)

After five years in Adelaide, we decided to move to Launceston in Tasmania, once again following the call in answer to a need! There was a small church in Launceston, needing a pastor, and we were ready to go. We did not know it at the time, but here God would teach us some vital lessons in faith, and by assimilating those lessons we would gain two miracle sons!

One lesson of faith came through our reduced income. We went from a secure equivalent of 70 dollars to an average of 25 dollars. Each week we paid the church bills first and what was left over was our wage for that week. But God was faithful and through his people, he made provision for us. We would find boxes of groceries left on the front verandah and bank cheques in the letter box. These continued to arrive until the time we were able to gain an adequate wage.

After Sharon's third birthday, I began to feel the urge to become a mother again. It was an enormously strong desire, and we began to pray about it. On the surface, it seemed madness to attempt another pregnancy. I had spent so much time in bed, and had suffered so much to have Sharon, and now had two children to look after as well as a busy church schedule.

But I did become pregnant again, only to lose yet another child, once again at two months.

This time the specialist told me that from now on all my babies would terminate at two months. I had too many antibodies to bear a child, and in those days (during the 1960s), no one knew how to overcome this problem.

Ken and I spent some time talking this over. How could we continue to preach that Jesus was the healer if we could not have any more babies? If I hadn't wanted a baby there would be no problem; but I did! The God who gave me the yearning to have more children, and who allowed me to become pregnant, surely could work a miracle and help me to overcome this difficulty in my body.

I reasoned this way. If God did not want me to have any more babies, all he would have to do would be to close up my womb as he had with Rachel in Old Testament times. Since he had not done that, but had allowed me to get pregnant, to me was sure proof he would help me. He who had given me the desire for motherhood would also give me the baby I wanted so much.

Despite these rationalisations, I was not going to rush in and conceive again without a definite word from God. Not only was there a strong probability of another miscarriage, but now (said the obstetrician) my own life was at risk. I might die myself if I tried to have another baby! What I needed was the faith of God, an unwavering certainty that he was with me, and that I had nothing to fear in attempting another pregnancy.

Finally, after much prayer I said to Ken, *"If I discover another couple who have had a similar problem, and it is established that God intervened in their life, granting them a baby, then I will go ahead."*

We continued to pray. Some time passed then one day in the mail, we received a Healing magazine from the USA. In it was this testimony from an American physician, Dr William Standish-Reed:

Question: *"My wife and I have an RH incompatibility. As a result, my wife has lost her last two children by miscarriages. Do you believe that we can hope to have children? Or should my wife or I have an operation to prevent any further conception?"*

Answer: *"A very dear friend of mine, a minister, at one time had this same problem. When his wife again conceived, they faced long months of anxiety, wondering whether they would have a normal child, or even if she would be able to carry the pregnancy through to its entirety. At that time, I had been studying the church's ministry of healing. I advised the minister to lay hands on his wife daily, and pray in the name of Jesus of Nazareth, asking God to allow her to have a normal pregnancy and a normal child...It is my feeling that a pregnancy carried through with husband and wife praying together would produce wonderful results. The minister's wife had a normal child. Only God knows how he could "juggle the genes" to cause such a result."*

We were overjoyed! Here was the guidance for which we had been asking. We set ourselves to pray for each other. Every night Ken laid his hands on me and prayed for me; then I would pray for him. This seemed so right to us. God had answered our prayer and given us specific instructions through a medical doctor, which gave us the extra confidence we needed. For us, it was like another verse added to the Bible; a promise of healing with our names on it! God would do for us what he had done for others!

After some months, I became aware that I had conceived again. I was excited, though a little apprehensive. I rang my doctor and she was horrified, despite my assurance to her that this time all would be well. She examined me, and to my astonishment told me that I was already three months pregnant. She took some blood from me and had it tested. I still had my antibodies but they were not harming the baby. She took some of Ken's blood, but it had not changed.

In fact, nothing had changed! Except that against all probability, I was having a successful pregnancy, with no sign of losing the baby! She kept asking me what we had done, and I kept telling her that we had prayed about it, and God was giving us a miracle baby.

She was a Christian doctor, so she had to accept what was happening; even though, as far as she knew at that time, it was not possible. Later on, we were to discover that God had intervened to "juggle our genes" and to give us an RH-negative baby.

In due time, and without being obliged to spend even one day in bed, I gave birth to our second son, Eric, who is now 45 years of age.

While in hospital I spoke to my paediatrician, who was caring for Eric, and I asked him, *"Doctor, do you understand how this could have happened?"*

He admitted that he did not know, but he did give me a warning. *"This was a one in a million chance. Don't try to do it again. It won't work another time."*

God must have heard him and decided to do it again! Four years later our third son, Baden, was born. He is now 40 years of age and is a joy to us and a constant reminder that God can repeat his miracles whenever he pleases!

Now we were able to rejoice in our God who does all things well. Ken began to pray for others who had a desperate longing to bear children, but who for some reason were unable to conceive. There are many such testimonies, but the one I will share with you happened in Perth, Western Australia. Ken was preaching in a church there and had a sudden insight, a "word of knowledge", that there were two women in the congregation who wanted a child but were unable to conceive. Two young ladies came forward, weeping; one had been married six years, and the other eight years. God had cared for them enough to reveal their deep longing to a visiting preacher!

Ken prayed for them and then left Perth to return home. Ten months later, we received a letter from their pastor. They had both had baby girls. One delivered after nine months and one week, and the other after nine months and two weeks!

Why was God teaching us such mighty lessons of faith? Looking back, we can see that God was growing a teacher! It takes perhaps only five or ten minutes to grow an evangelist. Anyone who has been saved can become a soul-winner, burning to tell others about Jesus; but it takes God 20 years to prepare a teacher.

Chapter Six

Guidance From Across the Pacific! (1974)

The phone rang. It was after midnight and Ken dragged himself reluctantly out of bed. An excited voice came over the wire. It was our good friend Pastor Peter Vacca, calling from 600 miles away. He had been praying and had seen a vision of a map of the world with a light glowing in our city of Launceston. As he watched, the light spread all over Australia, then across to New Zealand, and then around the world.

Peter was so impressed and stirred by his vision that he had to ring us and let us know. Could we explain what it meant? Ken and I weren't sure, but we said we would certainly pray about it.

Around this same time, one of the ladies from our church travelled across to Perth, and while there she heard a prophecy that a tree would grow out of Launceston, and its branches would spread over Australia, then across to New Zealand, and on around the world. A remarkably similar prophecy! But some months would pass before we could understand what God was saying to us.

For twelve years, we had laboured in Tasmania, and through this period God had blessed us with great miracles, some of which are mentioned in my book, *Divine Healing, The Wonder and the Mystery*. Many people had found healing in Jesus' name, our own congregation was growing, and we had helped establish four other churches. They had been years of laughter and tears, sunshine and sadness, happiness and frustration. There had been both defeats and triumphs. Much had been done, but Ken was troubled by a feeling that he had not fulfilled the full purpose of God.

I believe the Lord himself caused this, for it made Ken seek God earnestly about what his future should be. God denied him complete satisfaction in local church ministry, because he wanted to draw him into a special path, a hard path, and one that would take great sacrifice.

Ken became sure that God wanted to speak to him, to direct him in some way, and that he would find the answer in the USA. I was not fully aware of all that my husband was going through, but I knew he was struggling and needed encouragement. When he mentioned that he wanted to go to America, I knew at once that this was from God. Ken booked himself in to a School of Ministry in Melodyland Church, California, and also into one on church growth at Schuller's Crystal Cathedral in Orange County. He was accompanied on the trip by other pastors who wanted to go to the same conferences.

For both of us this was unusual. It was a dramatic departure from our normal way of understanding God's will. Why go to the USA? Couldn't the Lord speak in Australia? Yet we both knew this decision came from God. My experience and Ken's in guidance had been fairly uniform until now. When we needed to know God's will, we spent some time reviewing the situation and writing down the facts. Then we would make a reasonable decision based on those facts, using scripture and the wisdom God had planted in us over the years.

Even then, it was only by a series of miracles Ken ever got to America. Perhaps Satan was standing against him, sensing that this was a turning point in our lives. Perhaps the enemy knew that something would come from this trip that would help in building God's kingdom. So we had to contend with opposition from some people, a lost visa that turned up at the last moment on a plane that was not scheduled to fly, a pilot's strike, and many other irritations from the enemy. Or perhaps they were from God, once more testing our faith?

This time God spoke to Ken so differently, in a way that he was not able to accept fully for a time, not until it began to come to pass. When he arrived in the USA, he was ready to give up full-time ministry. He had given the Lord 20 years of his life, and though God had been very gracious and taught him many things, he was deeply dissatisfied, feeling that something vital was lacking from his life. Perhaps it was time to find a new way to serve the Lord?

But what did God want him to do? How would those prophecies about the light and the tree be fulfilled? He was perplexed and unsure, yet still hopeful that during his time in America the Lord would give him insight, and enable him to make a decision. Did God want him to write the books he felt he should write? Did it matter? Was it important to God?

Supernatural revelation.

Here are two letters written to me after Ken's arrival in Los Angeles.

14th August 1974

Sweetheart,

The time is 11.00pm Wednesday and I have just returned to my room after attending the evening rally at Melodyland. The speaker was Agnes Sandford, and she was most entertaining – a sprightly and gay-hearted 75 year old! Her message was not focused on healing, but rather on the power of prayer in the areas of life – and particularly on prayer for the salvation and healing of the nation, its government, homes, and schools.

Melodyland is an extraordinary place. Each night this week, it has been packed to the doors with about 4,000 people, perhaps more. And, of course, through the day several hundred people have been attending the clinic sessions. Several sessions are being conducted at the same time, some for pastors, some for young people, some for women, some for Sunday school teachers. The delegates are free to choose which sessions they wish to attend.

The evening rallies are more like concerts than church rallies. They are run very professionally (although they allow time for worship and praise) each person on the platform is highly skilled, from song leaders, to announcers, to singers and instrumentalists, to preachers. No one has appeared amateurish or made a poor presentation. The lighting effects, the sound system etc. are all the best money can buy. The soloists and the instrumentalists are absolutely top class. The audience also behaves more like a concert audience than a church congregation. They applaud all the items and sometimes demand an encore. The preacher is applauded as he comes onto the platform and quite often during his sermon when he has made a statement that enthuses the people, he will be interrupted by applause. Some of the preachers have received standing ovations at various points in their sermons. But it all serves to create an atmosphere of excitement and of eager response to the Word of God. Certainly there have been scores of decisions and of people filled with the Spirit so far this week.

The study sessions through the day have been intensive and useful. There are at least 200 ministers and their wives attending the minister's sessions. God has been dealing with me. I was very depressed and restless for a couple of days and I felt driven to prayer. I'm sure Ralph Wilkerson had a word of knowledge about me today, although he himself did not know to which pastor he was speaking. Anyway, time will confirm whether or not the word he gave for "one minister in this group" was in fact me. In the meantime, God is slowly giving me answers. Because of this, I have cancelled arrangements I had made to travel down to Mexico on Friday with Leon and David. They will still be going, with someone else to take my place, but I want to take advantage of having the hotel room to myself to spend the day in prayer. I will have to forfeit at least some of my part of the combined fare but it will be well worth it if I can gain some definite guidance from God. Tomorrow morning I am having breakfast with Dick Mills and am looking forward to being able to share fellowship with him and his wife.

I am hoping a letter will arrive from you tomorrow or Friday. Don't forget to send photos of yourself and the children. Pray with me that the Lord will bring me home with clear and definite guidance as to his will for you and me and for the church. Please convey my love to Philip and Brian and to their families and to all the saints. I'm sorry I can't write more often or in more detail, but the programme is so demanding that it leaves little time or energy for letters. An ocean of love to you and the children, Ken.

(The prophecy given by Pastor Ralph Wilkerson was this: *"There is a preacher here who is thinking of leaving the full-time ministry. If you do that, it will be a very costly mistake. God has called you and still has a work for you to do. The Lord forbids you to go back into secular business."*)

Since Ken had been contemplating buying a small business in Australia, he had no doubt this warning was directed at him! So here was something different from the usual silent prompting of the Holy Spirit!

Three days later Ken wrote again.

17ᵗʰ August 1974

Sweetheart,

Some incredible things have happened to me since I last wrote to you. On Thursday morning, I had breakfast with Dick Mills, not with any attention of seeking spiritual counsel from him, but simply to thank him personally on Barry's behalf for all the books he has sent Barry. But while we were eating breakfast he suddenly received a word of knowledge about me, and he described with astonishing detail the spiritual struggles I had been undergoing, my present spiritual position, and what directions my ministry was taking and would take in the future. I was stunned. My mind as it were was falling apart! If I had been the kind of person who weeps easily, I would have howled like a smacked baby. (As it was, I must admit, I just calmly continued eating my muffins, and Dick did not know what a staggering effect he was having on me until it was all over.) He continued discussing my past present and future (with virtually no help from me) for about an hour, and he gave me several scriptures which he said were from the Lord, and which point out the directions the Lord wants me to take. I cannot share with you here what he told me, and in any case, I am still trying to absorb and evaluate it all, but I will tell you all about it when I return. Suffice it to say it was a stunning answer to my restless cry for divine guidance and it was a remarkable vindication of my belief that somewhere on this trip through America I would find the direction I was seeking from God about my future, and about the future of the work in Tasmania.

But I was admittedly not expecting the answer to come so quickly nor in such an entirely supernatural form. Praise God for his goodness.

After breakfast, I went back to Melodyland for the morning service, which every Thursday is a worship and healing service. Usually about three thousand attend but on this morning, the clinic delegates swelled the service to 3500.

Dick Mills had offered to take me to lunch also, so after the service, I met him once again, and he drove me off to lunch in his Chrysler. On the way to lunch Dick stopped at a book shop and staggered me a second time by telling me the day before (Wednesday) the Lord had told him to buy me $200 dollars' worth of books. At the time, Dick had no money, but during the day, a person who owed him that amount paid him. To Dick this was confirmation of God's will, so he insisted I choose books to the value of $200 (including freight cost to Tasmania) I uttered a few feeble protests, but it was obviously pointless to resist, so I did as I was told. The books are now on the way! What an incredible man! He has also given me several books and tapes, which I have with me. I am still trying to recover from it all! Praise God with me.

With all my love to you all, Ken.

Here is the outline of the prophecy given to Ken in Los Angeles by Dick Mills

1. Concerning my own personal attitudes.

   a) 2 Ch 15:7. *"But you take courage! Do not let your hands be weak, for your work shall be rewarded..."* An exhortation to boldness, which

Dick linked with a prayer that I might be delivered from the fear of man.

b) 1 Co 15:58. *"Therefore, my beloved brother, be steadfast, immovable, always abounding in the work of the Lord, knowing that in the Lord your labour is not in vain."* A declaration that the days of difficulty are not yet over, but that eventually the full harvest will come.

c) He 6:9-10 *"In your case, beloved, we feel sure of better things that belong to salvation. For God is not so unjust as to overlook your work and the love which you showed for his sake in serving the saints, as you still do."* This was a rebuke of my dispirited feeling that God had forgotten me, that all my efforts had been largely in vain, which had led me seriously to consider resigning from the ministry (which Dick knew).

2. Concerning my future ministry.

a) Ecc. 6:9 *"Better is the sight of the eyes than the wandering of desire,"* A rebuke of my feeling that distant fields might be greener, and a demand that I be satisfied with a ministry based in Tasmania, plus a demand that I rejoice in the church God had raised up in Launceston and not be envious of other larger churches.

b) Re 3:7-11. This is a message addressed to the church in Launceston, and the church is to accept it as a special word from the Lord. But it is particularly addressed to me, for I am as "the angel of the church at Philadelphia" (Launceston). In this capacity, I must apply the particulars of this passage to myself. I should see the passage also as requiring I remain bold in exercising leadership in the assembly, within the framework of the role God has given me. However though I must retain a leadership role in Launceston I must be prepared to be less closely associated with the local church. In the fulfilling of this, and of the promise of an "open door," <u>I must keep myself ready for my ministry to take new and as yet undisclosed directions.</u>

After this stunning answer to prayer, Ken's depression lifted and he was able to enjoy the rest of the trip, learning many useful things for his future ministry. He came home to Launceston a new man, confident that he was in God's will to pursue the path to education and writing. Everything he had learned was put into practice slowly but surely. He spoke to his church council and they agreed to him spending more time in study and writing. They looked for an assistant to help with the church and Pastors Philip and Heather Baker were led to come from the Faith Bible College, New Zealand. Philip and Heather fitted in perfectly and the church continued to flourish.

From the age of 34, Ken had been studying for degrees in theology through Berean Christian College, Kansas, and USA. He believed that because of his writing ability, God wanted him to write books and he needed a theology degree to gain credibility. (This was stunningly confirmed by Dick Mills) As well as this, our church was continually losing our best young people to mainland Bible Colleges and they were not returning. Ken reasoned that there must be other pastors like him who would like to keep their young people and train them themselves. These different aspects came together in the idea of starting a correspondence college of theology. His trip to the States and his encounter with Dick Mills gave him the courage to go ahead with this plan knowing he was in God's perfect will for his life.

Chapter Seven

The Launceston College
of Theology is Born

By this time, Ken had his bachelor of theology and was studying for his masters in religious education through Berean Christian College of Wichita, Kansas. Later he was to receive a doctorate in ministry and then a Doctorate in Theology. We had worked out our logo, which sounded fantastic, though a little bold, *"The Whole Word to the Whole World."* The logo had a central circle with LCT forward and backward for Launceston College of theology with the words around the outside edge. Unfortunately, the LCT looked like the face of an owl, but even that fitted in because the owl was supposed to be a wise bird.

As remembered by Ken's first secretary, Mary Shadbolt, here is a description of the efforts she and our friends went to in typing and printing the books the old fashioned way. Praise God for all of the modern inventions which make printing so easy today!

Mary Shadbolt's memories of early days

It was in 1973 when I had some time on my hands that I offered my typing services to Ken Chant at the CRC Launceston. I saw he was a busy man, too busy to do his own typing. One day, instead of the usual work, a page of copy appeared on my desk entitled, "The Authority and Authenticity of the Bible. It was the beginning of the first unit of the Diploma Correspondence Course of the Launceston College of Theology.

Ken and Alison set me up with an electric typewriter in the basement of their house, giving me a supply of typing paper, a bottle of obliterator for my mistakes. Ken showed me how he wanted me to set out the paragraphs and to number them, then he left me to it. Page after page of handwritten work began to issue from his desk. When the church moved into their first property, The Georgian Chapel, we moved the office there. The writing continued, and we had completed "Great Words of the Gospel," "The Holy Spirit," "Healing in the Whole Bible," "Faith Dynamics," and "Throne Rights" by the time the church moved again into a larger property.

As the correspondence course grew, completed questionnaires began to flow in from delighted students who wanted to know and understand their Bible. This was too much work for a busy pastor, so my friend and working colleague, Lois Mackey was introduced to the task of marking the papers.

In 1975, Philip and Anne Marie Koopman started to help with the printing of the correspondence course. At first, the printer was situated in one of the bedrooms of their family home, but the course grew so fast, that their garage was converted into a printing room with the help of Jeff Merry and David Prentis, two of our church elders.

Anne would make all the masters for the printer. This consisted of making one master for each page of every book within the course. The master would only last for one print run of 500 pages. During the printing process, the masters could be damaged or smudged which would mean they would have to be typed all over again. The master printing machine, bought from a professional printery, was huge and worked similarly to a photocopier only much slower.

Once the master was made it was attached to one of the cylinders of the printer, and ink would be put into a tray and the master would be wound through to imprint on to another cylinder. A trial run of approximately 10-20 copies would be done to ensure the ink was consistent. Once the ink was correct, a run of 500 copies would be completed. Sometimes the printing would cause Philip great distress because of machine breakdowns, damaged masters or paper jams, which then interfered with meeting deadlines.

After the copies were printed, each page would be put into a collator that could hold up to nine pages. These pages would then be hand collated and placed in readiness for the next group to be attached to them. We had a dedicated group from the church who gave up their time to help with this task. When all the pages were printed and collated, and the covers were in place, the books were ready to be bound. A run of 500 books could take a week to a week and a half to complete in this fashion with many hours of manual labor being required.

The attitude of all the helpers was one of shared love, spiritual well-being, and an understanding of the great work that was being achieved. No one received any pay for the work they did; it was all done voluntarily for the glory of God. Because of this, we could charge quite a small amount for each book. The first lessons therefore cost the students only $15.00 each.

Philip and Anne continued to print for a period of three years and in that time, there were 15 correspondence course books, which were fully printed, collated and bound over and over many times. Their eleven year old daughter, Andrea, would always help with the collating and binding, and she also helped her father if there were any printer problems, especially when smaller hands were needed to get out the paper jams. They did all this with the love of God in their hearts and they dedicated their time free of charge to the betterment and understanding that came with doing the course. (We tried many different ways of producing the books over the years but finally in 1990 decided to use a Photo Copier as in this way we could make only the books we needed each week and did not have to store too many. Now our American office has the books printed by one of the largest printers in the USA, who with their new machinery can offer to print from one book to hundreds, depending on the order).

Our Bible correspondence course is born!

So the Bible Correspondence Course was born in 1974. We began with nothing, no money, no equipment, but with a group of wonderful people, our friends in Launceston, who were willing to stand with us, work hard, and sacrifice to make our vision possible. As each new book was written our student body grew, until now (2012) the books have gone into more than 150 different countries, several of them have been translated into other languages, and thousands of people have been taught and enriched by them.

After some years of gradually increasing numbers of students enrolled, we were able to print one of our most successful advertisements

"Why Write An Ad When You Get Letters Like These."

- "The units are beautifully written" (An Anglican priest).
- "A most eloquent and comprehensive course." (A student).
- "The books are very exciting. I have just finished Great Words of the Gospel...I believe the article on justification is the best I have read." (CRC pastor).
- "I would like to express my appreciation for this fine Bible course. It is both exciting and challenging." (A student).

- "We have been delighted with the preparation and concepts contained in the first unit." (Salvation Army Captain).
- Thanks for a fantastic course," (A student)

These comments reflect the impact made on the lives of hundreds of people throughout the nation by the Diploma Correspondence Course of the Launceston College of Theology.

This same attitude was reflected in an article in a Tasmanian newspaper *The Northern Scene* Tuesday May 2nd 1978. This is part of a longer article by Mary McNamara.

Miracles, Exorcism His Business

"Cameron Street on a sunny morning does not seem to be the right place to be talking about the supernatural, of speaking in tongues, or exorcism. The discussion was taking place inside the Christian Revival Crusade Centre, and the man who was doing most of the talking was the Rev. Ken Chant. Mr. Chant is a CRC minister, and also the founder of the Launceston College of Theology, which, as he explained is an entirely different side of his spiritual business.

"The college was founded three years ago, and now has more than 1,000 correspondence students all over Australia and from as far afield as New Zealand, North America, and Britain. The course offered is one that makes the boundaries of denominations irrelevant. It is for charismatic Christians, and the students are from a great number of different churches.
Charismatic Christians believe that the supernatural phenomenon recorded in the ancient churches is just as possible today as they were then......"

Chapter Eight

Vision Ministries

The visions of the light and the tree were slowly being fulfilled! However, while the program was born in Launceston, four years later the Lord showed us that the time had come to move into a larger sphere. The word from God came while Ken was attending a conference in Singapore. He was invited to join Vision Ministries, under the direction of Alan Langstaff. Alan was the founder of Temple Trust, an interdenominational body set up to bring co-ordination into the Charismatic Movement and to hold conferences to teach Christians about the Baptism of the Holy Spirit. Vision Ministries and Vision Bible College had grown out of the Temple Trust Conference Ministry. Ken felt strongly led to make this move.

Meanwhile, at home during my quiet time, God had directed me to a verse in Genesis.

> *"Behold, I am with thee, and will keep thee in all places whither thou goest, and will bring thee again into this land; for I will not leave thee, until I have done that which I have spoken of." (Ge 28:15)*

I underlined this verse, not realising then its significance, but knowing the Lord had a message in it just for me.

When Ken arrived home from Singapore, the Lord quickened the verse to me again, and I went to look it up. I had no doubt the Father was leading us, and the time had come to move. So we shifted house to Sydney, and we both joined the staff of Vision Ministries. Ken also was appointed principal of Vision Bible College. The two colleges combined and our name was changed from Launceston College of Theology to Vision Bible College. While in Sydney Ken completed five more books, since then he has added another 15. He is still writing in his 78th year! Altogether, he has written 15 booklets and 30 books, with two more in process. This does not include all of the magazine articles and sermons he has prepared for publication! This article about the move appeared in the Tasmanian newspaper *The Mercury* Saturday October 7th 1978

Bible College Move

"A Launceston clergyman is transferring his inter-denominational Bible Correspondence College to Penrith, Sydney.

The Rev Ken Chant, first State chairman and supervisor of the Christian Revival Crusade's Launceston College of Theology will move at the end of next month. He said yesterday that he was moving the college to Sydney because of greater access to international teachers and preachers.

'The college has expanded so much since I first started it earlier this year that facilities here have been overwhelmed.'

The new college will comprise a residential hall, administration, lecture theatre, study rooms and extensive library. Our main goal is to develop a worldwide institution, which will attract students from overseas. 'At present we have 1,300 correspondence students studying basic courses in theology', said Mr. Chant. 'These include certificate, diploma, and degree courses in religion, Bible doctrine, and teaching, church history and structure.'

Staff for the college will mainly be Christian Revival Crusade ministry volunteers.

Since Mr Chant came to Tasmania 16 years ago, he has established six Crusade Centres in the State, with steadily growing congregations of more than 800 people altogether. He thought there was a great need in Australia for an interdenominational Bible correspondence institution."

After 16 years it was a very sad to leave all of our friends who had helped us so willingly. On the 8th January 1979, I wrote back to all of our friends in Launceston. Here is part of that letter.

Dear Friends,

Thank you all so much for your love shown to us during our last weeks in Tasmania and for the heartfelt farewells and the gifts, which we treasure as reminders of our dear brothers and sisters.

It was an added joy to have our son Dale with us on our last Sunday so that we were together as a family for our last grand farewell from the Launceston Assembly, our home church.

It was wonderful to have so many of you to wave to us and to hold streamers at the boat, but oh, so sad to see the tears of our dear friends. We watched Tasmania fade into the sunset while we shed a few tears ourselves, and then comforted one another...

We are very glad, now that we have arrived, that we are living here in Dick Street, Randwick, as it is much cooler than Penrith, the Lord knew best after all...

Lois arrived safely on Wednesday the 3rd January and it was so good to see a face from home and to hear all the latest news. Mary arrives on Saturday and we have her room all ready for her. She will have much work to catch up on, as we are now way behind in all the college work and this week Ken is away in Narrandera teaching at a short term Bible school so the work will be still further behind.

Please pray for us as next week we will be advertising the course at the Temple Trust Conference (run with the help of Vision Bible College students) and expect a big influx of students then.

Extracts from letters to Tasmanian friends 1979

Monday 12th February 1979

Dear Friends,

Well, the conference is over and all of the bustle and excitement of it ended. It was truly wonderful to be a part of such big meetings (15,000) and to see so many praising God at one time. I personally did not get to many meetings, as I was busy on our stall at the Expo of Christian books and colleges. We gave out hundreds of enrolment forms and there was great interest shown in our course, especially by the country people. Already we have noticed a big increase in enrolments, (almost double) and we have been kept busy in the office processing the new applications.

Lois has returned to Launceston after helping us for a month, we miss her very much but so far, we are coping, Mary is working very hard at her shorthand and managing very well...

It's good to meet our students everywhere we go and hear their eagerness to finish the course. One student told us she had been to Europe and left some of her books in Bulgaria. The people there were so thrilled to get them and are studying them. There is so much hunger in people to study God's word both here and overseas.

11th July 1979

Dear Friends,

Ken is just back from New Zealand where he visited our office at Whangarei and taught in the Bible School there.

As you know book ten "Angels and Demons" is printed now, some of our students have been waiting a year and five days for it! However, we do have some good news as Pastor Ray Gilmour has written a book for us on Creation...

We had our first graduation service on my birthday June 11th. Ken and Alan decided to put on their robes and be very dignified and the Dean, who is Church of England, wore his cassock, which is bright red. With his golden hair and bushy beard, he looked quite angelic.

Ken gave his Principal's address; also, one of the students gave a little thank you speech, which was good. Pastor Barry Chant was the main speaker and he was amusing in places but on the whole gave a very powerful message. At the end, he gave the students some scriptures, which in every case were absolutely right. Knowing each one as I did I was able to appreciate the way in which the Holy Spirit ministered to each one...

You may be interested to know that my mother was awarded the Order of Australia medal for her work with local government this year. She has received congratulatory letters from the Prime Minister and from the South Australian Governor plus many telegrams and letters from all over Australia.

One more thing and I think the most important of all. As you know when we moved to Sydney, we had to leave Lois behind and now we are losing Mary as well as she leaves for Africa sometime in August. We need your prayers for someone suitable to be found to do the typing and to supervise the office. So far, we haven't tried to get anyone but the time has come when we need someone badly. So please pray with us for this....

14th March 1979

Dear Friends,

Last Saturday Ken spoke at the Holy Spirit Seminar, which is held four times a year in Sydney at the Sydney Town Hall. On Saturday 500 people attended during the afternoon, 25 believers were filled with the Holy Spirit. The Sydney Ministers fraternal has organized these seminars since 1971 and many people attend from different denominations to receive the infilling. It has acted as a focal point for interested people for the last eight years. There are always new people each time so the influence of it spreads right through Sydney and has been of great help in establishing renewal in the churches. People tend to come for spiritual food until they have established renewal in their own churches and then they don't feel the need for it so much. Their places are then taken by others who have heard of what is happening and come to see for themselves

I received a tremendous blessing when I first arrived in Sydney. As the very first speaker, I heard repeated almost exactly the same words I had felt led to say to you all before I left Tasmania, namely, that God is going to move in a new and marvelous way in Tasmania and it would be through the ordinary people in the church and not necessarily through the leaders etc. The only difference of course was that this speaker was saying this about the whole of Australia. I got so excited that I wanted to leap up and say, 'That's what God told me!', but being me, I remained sedately in my seat, though inside I was shouting and rejoicing. He also said that God had revealed this to people in America and around the world, and everyone has their eyes on Australia to see what God is going to do!

This of course doesn't mean we can sit around and wait for God to do it. We should be all the more eager to make it happen knowing we are working with God, and that it is his time.

"A prophecy will not fulfill itself 'automatically' but only fulfill itself through men who act accordingly." ("Gifts and Ministries" Bittlinger pg.62)...

Many new and wonderful things are happening in the Bible College with some very gifted people offering to help Ken with his graduate programme. Next Friday some key personel are having a special "think tank" in order to come to some decisions regarding the future of the college. Please pray for us that God's will be done in everything.

April 1980 after a fact finding trip to the USA

Dear Friends

During our trip to the USA we were assured many times that the Diploma Correspondence Course was needed there. There is no other conservative, charismatic course such as ours. We hope to begin in July as there is a big charismatic conference then and it will be a good place to start. Please pray for this, that God will lead us to make the right arrangements, and find the right people to help us.

On our return, we received confirmation that we will have an office for the Diploma Correspondence Course in New Guinea and also in Southern India this year. Alan Langstaff has a vision that we will also go into Europe and even behind the Iron Curtain. Rev. Urquhart took a set of our books back to England so perhaps next year we will see an office established there.

The most exciting development this last few weeks has been an opening into Burma where we now have 7 students including one high up in the Anglican Church and a L't Colonel in the army. Evidently, no missionaries are allowed to stay there now and so the correspondence course has become a viable alternative for sound charismatic teaching.

Please pray for Ken that he will be able to complete Immanuel in the next four weeks.

He is due to go to Sri Lanka, India and Thailand in August/September to attend a conference and to teach and preach as well. Ken needs your prayers for God to preserve his health and strength, and for more helpers to get the work done before the doors close. I feel an urgency to move quickly over the next five years, who knows how much time is left to us.

The correspondence course continued to expand steadily.

In 1979, Alan and Dorothy Langstaff, with their children, moved to Minneapolis in the USA. Their goal was to expand Vision Ministries internationally. They invited us to join with them, saying that our correspondence course was needed there. Several American friends had also urged us to do this, because of the lack of a similar programme in their country.

After only two years in Sydney, we did follow Alan and Dorothy to the USA. We had moved to Sydney to work with Alan and head up his Vision Bible College and now he was asking us to move again, this time to USA. This was a big move, although the idea of taking the Correspondence Course to the USA was an exciting one. We had no idea how hard this move would be for all of us.

Chapter Nine

We Move to America

"Come on Mum, let's go. It'll be fun," clamoured our children.

My husband looked at me across their heads.

"It's your decision, Honey. I think we should go, but I'll wait until you feel this is right."

When any momentous decision had to be made concerning our family, Ken would just wait patiently, until either I agreed with him, or we both decided to drop the idea. He knew that if the decision he had made was God's leading, then God would also show me.

My spirit was in turmoil. How could I feel good about leaving my country, my oldest son, my parents, and the rest of my family, to go to the USA, perhaps for many years, perhaps forever!

Our daughter Sharon was 20 years of age; what if she decided to marry in the USA? What of our sons, Eric and Baden, their education, their future? For days and nights I walked up and down my living room, pleading with the Lord to show me his will.

One morning I left my bed early, agitated, and unable to sleep. I was kneeling in the living room of our home in Lillee Pillee, a suburb of South Sydney, exhausted from grappling with the thoughts that continually tumbled through my mind. In the still quietness of the early morning, God spoke to my heart. His voice was unmistakable, and so reasonable, so reassuring.

"You are trying to look too far ahead. Don't look ahead twenty years but just two years. I promise you that after two years you will either be coming home, or you will want to stay."

Enormous relief filled my heart! All my burden and anxiety vanished. Two years would be fun, an adventure to be enjoyed, not an imposition to be endured. I woke Ken and told him what had happened, and he rejoiced with me at this unusual answer to my prayer.

Over the next few weeks, we said a sad farewell to our son, Dale, who was still pursuing his Ph.D. at Monash University, Melbourne, Victoria, and to our family and friends in Australia.

We didn't take much with us - Ken's books, some blankets, our clothing, and some silverware. Everything else we gave away.

Five days after our arrival in the USA, Eric became violently ill. We had noticed that he was not his usual brisk and happy self, but had thought this was a natural reaction to leaving his friends. Throughout the night, his condition deteriorated until, in the early morning, we had no alternative but to contact a doctor. The verdict was immediate. Eric was not even permitted to return for his toothbrush. Instead, he was rushed into emergency for an operation to remove his appendix!

Piling poverty on misery, we discovered that, for the first time in Ken's frequent trips overseas, no traveller's insurance had been taken out for us. This meant that only the amount covered by our Australian medical insurance was at our disposal. The difference was $2,100!

Right about now several people might question our trip to the USA, but I knew God had spoken to me, so we were not crushed. In fact, this incident opened up the hearts of the American people to us in an exceptional way. We were given the loan of a car, and on our finding a suitable house, they showed their generosity by giving us the furniture we needed to set up our home. From several different people the money was given to us to pay Eric's medical bill. The Lord had turned a potential tragedy into a triumph!

Perils in a strange land

Just two months after our arrival in the USA, and shortly after settling into our new home, Sharon and I drove Ken to the airport. He had a prior appointment to fly to Singapore to teach for two weeks at a Bible School.

By this time, we had bought a second-hand Oldsmobile, and Sharon had mastered driving on the right hand side of the road. She felt confident that she could find her way home after saying our goodbyes to Ken at the airport terminal. I did not feel competent as yet to drive, so I gladly yielded her the wheel. (In fact, two years passed before I grew brave enough for the freeways. Due to some strange proclivity, as a left-hander I continually mistake my right hand for my left!)

So Sharon took over, and soon she and I were on our way home. Only a mile down the road, the dashboard light warned us the engine was running hot. We pulled in to the nearest service station. In our innocence, we did not realise that this was just a gas station without a competent mechanic. We asked for help and the attendant lifted the bonnet and began to unscrew the radiator. Even I knew that was not wise! The cap shot into the air, and because of a slight tilt in my direction, the contents hit me in the face. Hot water mixed with anti-freeze is not the nicest combination to strike face and hair! Soaking, my eyes filled with the solution, I staggered to the ladies room and washed myself. Worse was to come!

The gas attendant filled up the car radiator again and insisted that we would have no more trouble. We drove off obediently, but barely a mile down the road the red light blinked again, and we knew that we would have to get help.

Panic seized me as we drove off the freeway. This was unfamiliar territory. The street seemed poor and unkempt. My memory began to stir with accounts of robberies and murders. The people all around us seemed unfriendly. We parked the car and I made Sharon lock herself in while I attempted to find someone to rescue us. I walked nervously down the street - remember I am an Australian, and I had read some lurid tales about America! I was convinced that everyone carried a gun, and would need little excuse to use it!

Finally, I reached a service station and asked to use the telephone. Imagine my horror when I opened the phone book and found not one of the people I knew listed. We lived in the Minneapolis part of the Twin Cities and we had driven into St. Paul. The people I knew were all in Minneapolis, and the service station had no telephone book for that city. Wet and cold from my dowsing, miserable and afraid, I cried out to God. Immediately he reminded me that only the Sunday before we had met a friendly couple from Texas, and they had given me their phone number.

"If we can be of any help, then let us know."

Those were the words that rang in my ears. Of course, they lived in St. Paul! Quickly I pulled out my pocket diary and found the phone number, my voice a little wobbly by this time.

Later, at home, showered and warm, I thanked God for his thoughtful provision. Of course, I thanked my Texan friends as well. They were truly used by God to rescue this timid Australian from her difficulty.

More prayers answered (1981-1986)

A week later, while Ken was still in Singapore, I became extremely ill with a hemorrhage. When it had not stopped after three weeks, Sharon telephoned the doctor. He advised her, if the bleeding continued beyond another hour, she should bring me into Emergency. Instead, she decided to call our Christian friend, Dorothy Langstaff. God heard our prayers, and half an hour later, the haemorrhage suddenly ended!

Ken's return from Singapore was a time of great rejoicing. We were about to experience our first Minneapolis winter, and it was good to know the head of the house was home. Our initiation into the mysteries of snow, icy roads, and frozen pipes was to begin with the worst winter Minnesota had suffered in 100 years!

One night Sharon went out to take a friend home. Because the car was warm, she neglected to take any heavy clothing with her. On her return journey, she became lost in a fog. Unless she found a service station soon she would run out of fuel and maybe freeze to death by the side of the road. She prayed for guidance as she drove slowly along. Almost immediately, she saw a gas station, and was able to fill up and return home safely. In our ignorance of the danger we had not been alarmed by her late arrival, but we praised God that we had taught our daughter to pray and seek guidance from him.

Since our arrival in the USA, six months earlier, three of us had faced a threat of death, and more was to come. Why was God allowing these things to happen?

I walked into our office one afternoon to find Ken in excruciating pain. He was doubled over and the perspiration was streaming down his face. I touched his forehead and it was cold, then almost at once, he became extremely hot. *"What is it,"* I cried.

"I've been having these bouts of pain for some time. I'm not sure what they are," he groaned.

"You must go to the doctor and have a check up. You owe it to your family!" I argued. It was frightening to see my strong husband in such pain. We prayed together and then made an appointment for him to see a physician.

The doctor's verdict was that the pain was caused by cancer, gallstones, or an aneurism. A day was set for an x-ray. Meantime Ken was prayed for by two of his friends, Pastor Alan Langstaff and Pastor Rod Lensch. They agreed together that whatever was causing the pain would be healed. I was still full of apprehension. What would I do if Ken were to die? I prayed earnestly, but my mind was in a ferment. I could get no peace. God was unable to speak to me because I was unable to hear his voice. Then one morning, very early, I woke suddenly. This verse of scripture came into my mind, and I knew immediately that God was speaking to me - *"With long life will I satisfy him and show him my salvation"* (Psalm 91:16).

Immediately I knew Ken would live, that whatever had gripped him was undone. I had been given the faith of God, which nothing can shake!

Ken went in for his x-rays and the doctor was amazed, he could find nothing wrong. Quickly he took another x-ray and once again, it showed nothing. This occurred forty years ago and he has had no more trouble since then.

Learning God's purpose

Now we had to face the fact that four of the family had had life threatening experiences in our first year in America. Why had this happened to us? Had we missed God's guidance? As we pondered the matter, we remembered that during our three years in Sydney we had not had to believe God for anything. Everything had come easily to us; consequently, our "faith muscles" had grown very feeble. We could see plainly that God had now put us through a crash course. He needed to have us tough, and resilient in faith, not flaccid and weak. He had brought us through, as he always does when we trust him totally to keep us in his will.

The end of the two years arrived and, true to his word, the Lord gave us the opportunity to return to Australia. By that time however I was happy to stay. I realised that we had only begun to scratch the surface of the work that we had to do in upgrading and re-editing the correspondence course for the American market.

Our move to the States we thought a failure at first as we had difficulty getting the correspondence course off the ground. Two or three times we were offered nation wide coverage only to have this removed again. Once it was a nationwide TV show that later decided to begin its own course, then it was a group who offered to make Ken famous if he would give them a percentage of the collections from his preaching. He realized this would make him a virtual slave, having to do their will, and he felt this was not right in God so he refused. Last of all, a group began televising Ken coast to coast and then promptly went bankrupt and had to come off the air. Obviously, God had other plans; there was a different path he wanted us to go. He wasn't finished with Ken yet, wanting to make sure that success would not destroy him.

Then after five years in Minneapolis and very little result from all our efforts to spread the Correspondence Course we were asked to begin a Bible School in San Diego. We were offered many things we needed to make the course viable in the USA so we accepted the call, not realizing that we were to enter five years of struggle in the midst of which Ken's character was to be savagely attacked. God did defend him miraculously as he was proved innocent of all charges and a public apology was given and received.

Seven more years were to go by before we were to return to Australia, and before the last part of the verse God had given me in Tasmania was to be fulfilled. But that is another story, an unfinished one! God is in control and that is all we need to know.

Chapter Ten

Our Move to San Diego

Our first calamity occurred on our way to San Diego to start the Bible College. The journey was fraught with danger. On the way, Ken was almost crushed to death between our moving truck and a tree, and then when we arrived in Riverside, California, everything was stolen from us. I told our friends all about it in my newsletter of September 1984.

Dear Friends,

Everything was stolen! All our personal possessions, Ken's library notes, the files and stock of Vision College – everything!!!

We were stunned and for a time we just could not believe it!

Our journey across to the West Coast had given us the opportunity to see this big country as never before. It was a relief to have finally done with the chaos of house moving, with the shutting and locking of the door to our hired removal van. The dolly, which held our daughter's small Chevette sedan, was securely hooked up behind and by late Monday afternoon we were ready to head out West – the beginning of our 2,000 mile trek.

For the first day and a half we traveled the Great Western Plains through very lush country (acres of growing corn stretching for mile upon mile) right through to Denver and then on to the Rocky Mountains. This brought us quite a contrast to the flat country as we traversed fold upon fold of mountains. The scenery here was very beautiful. Then began the dry places – spectacular scenes across the colourful Colorado terrain, on and on through hundreds of miles of arid country. Utah, Arizona, Nevada, with each place having a special beauty.

Ken had planned for us to spend our last night in transit at Riverside, California, thus leaving us a very easy drive to El Cajon (where a house, provided by the San Diego church was waiting for us). Hopefully we would arrive refreshed and ready for the unloading and relocating of our belongings in our new home... Up until this moment, everything had gone beautifully – just like a dream. But that dream was soon to be turned into a nightmare.

Saturday morning, after we had breakfasted, our son, Eric, who had done the bulk of driving of the truck) went to check it out before we set forth. He came back to us with a rather shocked expression on his face to tell us that the truck had gone! Ken went to look and sure enough, everything had gone – lock, stock and barrel, from the well lit, security guarded, hotel parking lot.

We immediately contacted the police who took full particulars and advised us to stay on another 34 hours before driving, in our other car, to El Cajon – just in case there was a sighting of our moving van. When there wasn't, we came on down, rather shocked to be left with only the few traveling clothes we had set out with for our long journey.

During this period of waiting Ken was as white as a sheet, trying to come to terms with the loss of his library, 32 years of sermon notes, his books and manuscripts, and revelations God had given him, all lost. I grew quite worried as he sat at the table in the kitchen, bereft of his tools of trade, his whole life's work. The rest of us had suffered too, but for Ken it was truly a bitter blow. One he had to work through in prayer, and he did. It took him a week but, not long after he said a resigned, "Yes Lord, if you want me to begin again then I am willing," the police phoned us.

On Thursday August 30th, we received the call from the Riverside police to say the truck had been found – minus the dolly and Chevette. We went up to Los Angeles to claim what was left behind by the thieves. It was with great rejoicing that we found a huge mound of books and papers in the back of the truck (there was little else). It was all such a mess but we worked on through the day packing into more than 50 boxes, what proved to be the bulk of Ken's library and files, which were the result of his 32 years of ministry that God has built up through the years.

That had been our main cause for concern, together with all the materials and files pertaining to the Diploma Correspondence Course. Most other items could be replaced (with the exception of those things that held sentimental value for us. But the things of God were our tools of trade, and so we were rejoicing at the goodness of God in restoring them to us so that our work could carry on as before – a little slowly at first, but practically unhindered. It seems that Satan tried to defeat us, but God showed himself to be the victor – praise his mighty name!

We are slowly settling in. The folk at South West Christian Centre where Ken has taken on the position of Principal of their newly formed College of Ministry, have welcomed us with open arms, and hearts. Their support has been total. It is surely a joy to be among God's praising people, to feel an immediate sense of being "at home." We know God has much for us here, and for the body. We are even more excited at what God is going to do in our midst than we were when we left Minneapolis.

And so it is with much thanksgiving that I write to you, sure in the knowledge that God is with us, and will continue to bring much blessing to you through the DCC....

*More extracts from letters October 1984 – Jan 1989

Dear Friends,

We have several good things to report.

First, we are pleased to tell you that prayer has been answered for some of our goods that were stolen. Our daughter's car that we were towing has been found by the police, with its contents intact. The car was not damaged at all. So we have regained a few things, for which we praise God! Thank you for your prayers.

Secondly, we have been approached by some pastors in Indonesia who want to translate the DCC into Indonesian for training Indonesian pastors. There is a great need there and we would ask your prayers for the translators.

Here in America we have been in contact with a prison Chaplain who has asked for a set of the DCC books to teach the prisoners in his care. He told us that many of the prisoners are coming to the Lord and then going out to work for God when their time in prison is completed. We have heard that the same thing is happening in the prisons in England. God is working among prisoners in a very real way and proving his power to save and deliver.

On October 26th, Ken and I will be leaving for Scotland where the Rev, David Black is preparing to launch the Diploma Course in Britain. Faith Dynamics and

Christian Life are the first two books, which will be printed there. We wait with interest to see what God has planned for the DCC in the British Isles.

During our stay, Ken will be speaking in several different Bible Colleges and churches throughout the country, namely Glasgow, Sussex, Kent, London and Cornwall.

During our absence Mrs. Pat Eades, who has come to assist us for a time, will be acting as registrar and taking care of Vision College for us.

Please continue to uphold us and the work in prayer...

It was around 1985 that we met and joined forces with Dr. Stan DeKoven, but that is his story and I will let him tell it in his own way later on in this history.

Letter March 20th 1986

Dear Friends,

So much had happened since our coming to USA that I feel I could write a book!

We have certainly had some adventures since our arrival...This past year has been traumatic with the pastor of the church here in San Diego having to resign, and our invitation to take over the church.

The last six months have been hard but extremely rewarding, as we have sought to bring the people through an exceedingly difficult and painful time. Now God is blessing the church more and more and we look forward to a wonderful future.

Ken and Scott McKinney, from International Evangelism, and several members of our congregation were used mightily in the Philippines last November. They were there for ten days and Ken taught around 250 pastors and leaders through each day. Then in the evenings,

Scott spoke at an evening rally with up to 3,000 people attending. Blind eyes were opened and at least two deaf and dumb people were delivered with many other miracles occurring. Ken and Scott are planning another similar outreach to Pakistan in October this year.

God has placed us here in this church through a series of circumstances and we could not refuse the task. God has kept us here through a series of miracles and we are content to remain as he wills...

Ali and Frances Duran, members of our church, are in charge of our Mexican outreach. Ali used to be a spiritualist medium; her mother was one and also her grandmother. But God miraculously delivered her and now she is a missionary to the Spanish people, able to tell them that they too can be delivered from evil superstition and occult practices. Ali and Frances travel to Mexico regularly with food and clothing that is collected here. Frances is a mechanic and he is also able to restore old cars and trucks for the mission stations. They visit and help support ten mission stations altogether. Mexico is so poor and most of the people live in abject poverty. Sometimes just in holes in the ground! We Christians cannot live so close (20 miles from the border) and not do something to help.

Our church here is also interesting in that we have such a diversity of nationalities. We have Mexicans, Indians, Philippinos, Black Americans, and people of mixed race, Whites, and even half a dozen Aussies. But altogether we are brothers and sisters in Christ and no one feels any different to another. We are of one blood in Christ!

Letter March 3rd 1987

Last week I had the pleasure and excitement of preaching through an interpreter for the first time. It was an enjoyable experience as it gave me time to think between each sentence or two...Mexico is a very important and strategic land for the USA and we need to pray and intercede for the people of that land. It would be a tragedy if Mexico became communist.

Along with this letter, you will see a note concerning a four month programme we are beginning here in August. We have been asked to do this by Logos Bible School with whom we are affiliated.

January 24th 1989

Dear Friends,

Ken is today teaching at Christ for the Nations...Now that we are no longer pastoring the church in San Diego, we will be entering a new phase of our ministry. Ken will be traveling more and teaching in various places. Each weekend of February is already taken up. Also, we will be starting our first 18 week course of Bible College in San Diego. This will be an intensive course for those students who would like to get a thorough grounding in the Bible as quickly as possible. Our first intake begins on the 6th February and ends on the 2nd of June.

After the graduation, Ken and I will be spending 6 weeks in Australia and New Zealand. The next 18 week course will begin in August.

Because we have had so many calls recently to Africa, Pakistan, India, Indonesia, the Philippines and Mexico we are beginning to feel like missionary teachers. We cannot do all that needs to be done without any help from our friends so we have decided to reactivate our Vision College Foundation (which gives people opportunity to give money to help with the distribution of books into third world countries).

Teaching is so important in third world countries, especially in Africa where people are running to the altar by the hundreds to accept Christ. But if there is no one to teach them and no literature to read they tend to mix their Christianity with their tribal beliefs and soon fall away or get into heresy.

We are in touch with one of our graduates in Africa who is now preaching and teaching and building churches. He and others are pleading with us to visit them for Crusades and to teach groups of pastors.

Chapter Eleven

Called Back to Australia 1989

"God, please tell us what to do and we'll do it. Whatever it is!"

This was an exasperated cry from the bottom of my heart. I was truly frustrated and bewildered.

Ken had suffered a stomach haemorrhage and had to resign as pastor from the San Diego church. The years of trying to pastor the church and still take care of the DCC as well as continue to write his books had taken their toll and he was exhausted. Initially we both thought we would go back to itinerate ministry but now God had closed the doors that were normally wide open to Ken.

It was around July 1989. For months, we had been praying for guidance as to what God wanted us to do next. Our house was on the market but not selling. Ministry opportunities had dried up. We felt as though we were in a cocoon of silence. We couldn't reach others and they were, seemingly, ignoring us.

Pastors and churches which normally were only too eager for Ken's ministry were strangely silent. We waited on God. Weeks went by, finally, in sheer frustration I decided to get a nursing job, which I did.

More time elapsed.

Meanwhile, Ken finished writing his book, *"When the Trumpet Sounds"* and because we needed guidance, so much ourselves he began writing a book on guidance *"Discovery."* I decided to add some of our stories of faith to this, some of which are repeated in this history.

How did we get ourselves into this position? We had resigned from our church in San Diego, feeling our time there was ended. We had been confident that we would receive plenty of itinerant ministry to keep us going. But, nothing, silence from everyone, and what was far worse, silence from God.

Every other time in our lives we had been fully confident of our next step but this time, NOTHING! Hence my cry, *"Tell us what to do!"*

A prayer written by me, and discovered recently among my papers, indicates just how desperate we felt at this time.

Heavenly Father,

Entering into your presence is like drawing honey from a rock, in you, all things are possible and what seems impossible to us is joyfully and freely possible with you, because you are our maker, our deliverer, our keeper.

Thank you for the past deliverances, healings, provisions, victories and miracles you have granted to us. We are grateful and our hearts are filled with joy because we trust you.

Lord, you see all and know all, I pray that you will not allow our enemy to triumph over us but that you will make provision for us and for the Bible College.

We pray for the future of the Bible College and for provision and accommodation for us and for Logos. We pray for the students, give them provision also, Lord, that they might meet their obligations and give you glory in doing so. Give each one a ringing testimony to your faithfulness.

For the other pastors we are in the process of contacting, we pray for guidance and wisdom in the steps we take and the decisions we make together. Give us favour and glorify your name in all that we do.

Grant wisdom to Ken and others tomorrow as they discuss our future plans. Reveal your will and purpose I pray.

Remember in all things we trust you and as we do your will, we know you will provide. We accept your testing and your discipline. Our only desire is to glorify your name, to exalt you and to train people to be better servants for your work in your kingdom,

Hear this prayer from my heart 18th April 1989.

Then in September, I received word that my mother had had a stroke, and of course, I made plans to visit her in Australia. While there, I was amazed at the number of pastors and leaders who were anxious for Ken to return to Australia. We had thought there was no place for us in Australia; because we had been gone so long, we thought we were no longer needed. I mentioned this to Ken on the telephone and he prayed about it and after a week of waiting on God, made the decision to return.

After nine months of stagnation as far as selling our house was concerned, that very week we had a buyer who made us an acceptable offer on the house.

Was God waiting for us to make the decision to return to Australia? Had he shown us that is what he wanted but we hadn't listened?

Whatever the reason, the experience certainly gave us some new views on guidance, which have become a great blessing to many people.

Is it possible that God was giving us the option to stay in U.S.A. or leave for Australia? Perhaps he was, but I think he did want us to return to Australia for three reasons:

First: He had given me a scripture years before that we would return to our homeland. Then

Second: He had caused ministry to dry up for us in the U.S.A. (Invitations to return to the U.S.A. began to come in immediately when we returned to Australia. If we had had those invitations before we left, we would have stayed in the U.S.A.).

Third: God opened up the hearts of the people of Penrith Christian Fellowship Center to take care of us. Without their invitation and offer of housing and transport, we could not have returned to Australia.

So we came back to our home country early in 1990. Since then, new ministry opportunities have opened to us abundantly, both in Australia and overseas. Indeed, we have never before enjoyed ministry so much as we are now, nor has our ministry together ever been more fruitful. So in the end the guiding hand of our Lord proved sure and certain. As David discovered, the Shepherd's way may sometimes lead into a dark and dismal valley, in which death threatens, but he will never abandon us there to perish. Rather, his rod and staff retain firm control, and with sure steps, he brings his sheep through the valley, into his promised pasture.

It was after our return to Australia that God gave us another idea, and *Bible School in a Box* was born with us sending ten manuscripts plus exams and notes, enough to teach a group of students for one year, to strategic men in other countries. This has been taken up by Dr. Steve Mills who has expanded it with modern science by using one CD to give the whole curriculum to men of integrity who will take it and use it to train and develop their students.

Already we see the results of this in the number of churches planted by graduates of these classes in many places around the world.

Then came the idea of summer or winter schools where a number of students get together for one week of intensive study to accelerate their learning. We are always open for the Lord to give us strategic ideas to help us get students equipped to serve him more quickly!

Looking back, Ken went through some traumatic struggles during our years in the USA.

One time he was preaching in Maryland and one night after the service, God dealt with him severely over several hours. Finally, Ken surrendered all his ambitions to make his course a household word and said in essence. *"If you and I are the only ones to read my books, Lord, I will be content to continue writing them."*

He went through another traumatic time when God spoke to him through Robert Schuller and made him realize his ambitions were not God's ambitions.

Finally, the Lord brought Ken to the place where he handed everything over to God to do, as he wanted. Only when all of Ken's personal ambitions were destroyed was God able to go ahead with spreading the college worldwide through the work of Stan DeKoven and other dedicated men of God.

It was not until our seventh year in the USA, right in God's timing, that we contacted Stan DeKoven and the rest is history. We were able to leave Stan in charge and return to Australia to continue the work there.

We received a last word from Dick Mills when we were called back to Australia on May 27th 1989

"Betty and I pray that you will get clear guidance and direction without any static distractions.

- Is 30:21 *"Clear direction."*
- Pr 3:5-6 (Moffats) *"He'll clear the road for you."*

- Pr 16:3 (Amplified) *"He'll cause your thoughts to agree with his will."*
- Is 48:17 (NIV) *He's looking out for your best interests.*

"Ken and Alison I keep getting these words. The death of a dream that greater works might be done."

Pr 11:24 (Living Bible) *"It's possible to release it and grow richer and it's possible to hold on too tightly and lose everything."*

"We pray for your continued health, happiness, and fruitfulness." (Dick and Betty Mills).

Over the years, we had many prophecies given to us but we did not realize what they meant until many years later. Some had more than one fulfillment or were fulfilled over many years. It is hard for us to see God moving; it is only as we look back that we see what God meant in the word given.

One prophecy, in particular, we have only seen coming to pass in the last few years. At the time it was given we had no idea of the wonderful breakthrough the Lord would give the college in the future. It was a powerful prophecy given by Emanuele Cannistraci in San Diego on the 22nd June 1986.

"I did not bring you to this city (San Diego) just to become a pastor of another church and to remain in the comfort zone, for I have taught you, and I have created in you deep desires. And you have a noble discontent. But it is terrible this discontent that I have put in you. You are scornful of all that is phony, and weary of unreality, and you have been grieved by all of the religiosity that you have seen. And you have come to the place where you have said, 'My spirit is weeping; I must see reality!'

"O man of God, you will see reality. You are going to witness a people that are pure and holy. You are going to witness a people who have come out of Babylon, who will have nothing to do with its whoredoms, religious or otherwise. You are going to see a people who have made me Lord, Master, King, and the centre of their lives.

"You are going to be a dispenser of Kingdom truth and reality. In place of man centred religion, in place of humanism, you are going to preach the Kingdom of God coming in glory and power. You are going to preach the Government of God, the rule of God. You are going to teach the people Kingdom principles, and they will be brought under the authority of the Kingdom.

"You have labored, and you have toiled, and you have not seen the fruit of your labours. But let me tell you, O man and woman of God, there is coming a breakthrough in your life and ministry. Get ready for that breakthrough, says the Lord."

When you hear prophecies like this and then nothing seems to happen you put it to one side wondering all the while, what it means. We re-read it today in 2012 and concede that after twenty years we can see what God meant! Because of the wonderful men of God that he has raised up to spread the college to over 150 countries, and because of the recent development of our graduates going out to build churches we see the breakthrough we have so long desired.

A Summary of Our Life in the USA

The following information gives some idea of the gradual growth of the college over the years, and we know much more has been accomplished since then and much more is to come in the future.

Our 9-10 years in the USA were spent studying, updating the correspondence course, teaching, preaching, and pastoring. We had a busy time. Ken earned his doctorate in theology, and I a bachelor degree in Biblical Studies. The correspondence course is all reformatted. Ken has rewritten his book on the return of Christ, more from a moral and ethical viewpoint than the eschatological angle. He has called it. "When the Trumpet Sounds". He still needs to rewrite The Holy Spirit, expanding it into two volumes. One, the "Baptism in the Holy Spirit," and the other one the "Gifts of the Spirit." Also he intends writing one more book on Christology -- based on the book of Hebrews and the heavenly ministry of Christ.

Correspondence Course Update

Over the last fifteen years we have had over 5,000 students enroll in the course worldwide. There have been more than 1,000 graduates, 40 of whom are in fulltime service for the Lord, with many more serving God in positions of leadership.

Note: The student body has now expanded far beyond this; it is now almost impossible to ascertain how many have been blessed and educated in the Word of God through what is now Vision University. We have now many godly partners and authors who allow us to use their books as we allow them to use ours. This ensures that God's work is accelerated. The word for this age is "networking," men and women of God working together to accelerate the building of the kingdom of God.

We have sent out over $15,000 worth of Scholarship materials to students in countries such as Zimbabwe, Nigeria, India, The Philippines, Indonesia, Iran and Germany. Also too many prisoners here in Australia and in the USA.

Some translations have been completed and Dr. Stan DeKoven of Logos Bible College International, who is looking after our students in USA, is currently arranging to have the books translated into French for French speaking Africa.

Future Goals

We are negotiating to have the course distributed in England through Harvest Bible College in Birmingham...

We would like to set up a Graduate School of Ministry for those interested in further study by extension. We will be able to offer degrees through the American College, Logos Bible College International.

Ken may begin a newsletter, geared to pastors and leaders, sharing the information and insights he has gained over the past 40 years of ministry both in Australia and overseas.

Prayer Partners

We would like to thank those of you who have faithfully prayed and supported us over the years. Don't stop praying! God has a plan to fulfill. We may come to the end of our own resources, and we have many times, but God is able! His resources are inexhaustible. We pray that we may be able to continue to teach and to make our materials available to more and more people.

In Africa there is a great hunger for teaching as thousands come to know the Lord. They are crying out for teaching materials. We have recently given permission for our books to be printed in Zimbabwe where Pastor John Maxwell, one of our scholarship graduates, has set up a ministry.

In Asia, also they are crying out for teaching. The correspondence course fills a need as those who understand English, read, and learn, and then preach what they have learned in their local language.

From a Brochure Written in April 1990

"The harvest is so great, and the workers are so few,"
Jesus told his disciples. "So pray to the one in charge of
the harvesting, and ask him to recruit more workers for
his harvest fields." (Mt 9:37-38 Living Bible).

Diploma Course

Ken and I have been involved for many years in the setting
up and distribution of the Diploma Correspondence
Course, a series of books written and or edited by Ken,
along with examinations, which have proved popular both
here and overseas.

The current progress of the course is exciting, as it has
grown from humble beginnings to reach out to many
different lands and peoples.

Scholarships

Up to this time, we have given over $15,000 worth of
scholarships to pastors who have been recommended to
us by missionaries on the fields of Africa and Asia. There
are many more who are pleading for teaching. God is
doing a mighty work of conversion in these areas, but
many of the local pastors lack the teaching, which is so
essential to maintain converts in their new found faith.

A Remarkable Opportunity

This year the Lord has given us a remarkable opportunity
which will lead to us having our books printed at a greatly
reduced cost, thus enabling us to make more books
available free of charge to pastors in third world countries,
and also helping us to make the books more affordable
generally.

The church we are involved in here in Penrith has an
offset printer worth $20,000 plus everything else needed

to set up a print shop. Pastor Rob Thornton has made all of this available to us for printing our books.

Funds Needed

Our problem at this time is that the opportunities are outgrowing the resources! We need funds now to buy the necessary paper, ink, and chemicals to print the books.

We need funds also for some translations, and for further books to be written. Ken has more books he wants to write to complete the body of work for the DCC, and each book costs around $10,000 to produce.

Cost Effective Missionaries

If you could look on the books of the DCC, in a sense, as you would look on a missionary, then you would see that they are going out into other countries to spread the word and to teach the people. However, unlike their human counterparts they do not need a wage! This makes them very cost effective teachers of the Word. Indigenous pastors who can both read and understand English can study the books and then go out to preach to their people, in their own tongue, the things they have learned.

Support

If you are able to help financially and would like to share in this ministry then please do so...If you are unable to help financially, then we covet your prayers that God will enable us to raise the money that we need to do the work we feel he has commissioned us to do.

Meantime may the blessing of God rest on you and yours as we work together in his vineyard.

Your sister in Christ, Alison Chant.

25th July 1990

Dear Friends,

Sydney is beginning to feel like home to us now; the people have been very kind to us... Ken has begun a new book "Mountain Movers," a book on faith and answered prayer... Eric is steadily improving his printing techniques. He is learning more every day, and he is quite skilled enough now to begin printing our books...Our friend Barry Tombs, who has been providing us with all of the printing machinery, is starting to catch the vision of what we want to do. Because of this, he has provided us with an updated plate maker, which will give us much better print... God is good and eventually we will get everything prepared. Please continue to pray for us as we do for you. We have definitely left part of our hearts in the USA.

1st November 1993

Dear Friends,

First of all, we need to let you know that we are continuing to seek full accreditation with TRACS (Transnational Association of Christian Schools. We already have associate status, which means we have provided TRACS with reasonable assurance that we comply with their requirements pertaining to doctrine, philosophy, morality and financial accountability.

They have asked us to change our name from Vision Christian University to Vision Christian College and this has been done in USA...

Chapter Twelve

Fellow Workers in Australia

In this chapter, we will finish the Australian story with the story of Denis Plant who took over from Ken and Alison on their retirement from daily office duties, though not from writing which continues.

Dr. Denis Plant - Australia

In 1997 at the age of 67, I (Alison) announced my retirement from being Registrar for the Vision office! At that time, I was looking after Ken's father in his old age as well as doing the office work and keeping up with marking papers for the students. We were in touch with Pastor Denis Plant by this time as he had asked permission to start an Internet Bible College using our course. He had this up and running and asked us if he could take over the day-to-day running of the course for us as this, coupled with the Internet Bible college, would mean he could give up secular work.

Denis could not have accomplished all that he has without the help and support of his wife Roslyn and the office skills of Patricia and Steven Hart. These folks have worked together to continue to expand the college for us in Australia since our retirement from the main office.

Now thirteen years later Denis has spread our vision concept to many countries, including Burma, Nepal, New Guinea and South Africa. Denis has travelled extensively overseas and is never happier than when he is spreading Vision College and with it, the Whole Word to the Whole World. Here is his story.

Denis' Story In His Own Words

I have been in ministry in one form or another since a few weeks after I was saved at the age of 17 in the town of Nottingham, England. The year was 1968.

Following what proved to be a prophetic word, I came to Australia in 1970 and after a stint in the Australian Army as a National Servicemen, and I settled in a church in Liverpool and subsequently entered Bible College.

Following a Missions meeting in a small NSW town, I felt a call to commit myself to missions and prepared with my wife to go to Korea, an option that fell through, and was invited to the New Hebrides. However, following a civil war, the island nation was renamed Vanuatu. For Anne and I it meant we were not going to be missionaries, but the seed of mission-work was planted and has stayed with me to this day.

As the doors to the mission field closed a new door opened, so I began formal Pastoral ministry in Scone, NSW with my wife Anne. We later moved to Orange in NSW and pastored for 4 years until Anne was killed in a car accident. With two small children to look after it, was clear that I should resign from the church; however, I continued in ministry over the next few years in various organisations: pastoring churches, running outreach and training programs within the church all the while working with disabled people at the Spastic Centre. Later I worked with those who had intellectual disabilities with Lorna Hodgkinson's Centre while at the same time teaching in and starting bible colleges.

In March of 1985, I married Rosalind and we settled with the Foursquare Church in Liverpool where I started a bible college. That later became the denominational bible college as their college had been closed for a number of years and there was a clear need for ministry training. (This too is a run-on; it needs punctuation and rewording)Three years later, I took a number of students from our college in

Liverpool to Papua, New Guinea on a mission trip to find that God was calling me to that Nation and for the next two years, I worked as the Principal of the Lighthouse Bible College in Madang, PNG. Meanwhile the Bible College I started in Liverpool became the Foursquare Denominational Bible College known as LIFE Bible College.

During my time in Papua New Guinea, I decided to undertake studies with Vision Colleges. This was my introduction to Vision and I completed my Diploma of Theology through them and introduced Vision to the college in New Guinea.

I returned from PNG with a distinct vision from God - to put a bible college on the internet, an amazing concept for me as at that stage I had not so much as sent an email nor had need to receive one. I was truly internet ignorant. But God had a plan; I was motivated and driven by him! I began to study, seek help and advice and within six months had the framework of a Bible college on the internet - except for one small item. I did not have any subject matter. I had written and compiled many subjects but not being content with them, I needed something recognised, something that was credible, something that I knew could change people's lives and have the credibility that I believed was needed. This was God's work, not a hobby.

During a CRC Pastors river cruise, I met up with Ken; at this stage, I hardly knew him. We had met barely half a dozen times and always rather briefly. Out of interest he asked what I was doing and I told him and of my dilemma. Although I had the framework for the college ready, I needed to find the right material, and he offered his studies.... "Why not use Vision?" It was a "God moment" and I knew it was right. Ken promptly gave me all of his material on disks in WordStar. Soon I was converting them to Word and then discovered Adobe. The material could be securely sent over the internet without risk of being altered.

I should point out that at this stage there were no Bible Colleges on the internet that were offering courses, at least as far as I could discover. It was possible to go to an internet site and view colleges and their offerings, but you could not do more than enrol. I effectively pioneered the concept of an on-line bible college and was involved in the birthing of online learning.

About a year later I was joined by Patricia (Trish) Hart and after a couple of years her husband Stephen without whom we could not have seen the colleges grow to the extent that they have.

In late 2000, Ken told me that he wanted to retire. He had said so three times prior to this, and I had simply noted the fact but said nothing, but this time I was prompted to respond. "If you would be comfortable to do so I would like to take on Vision, provided you remain on as the President".

Ken agreed and we set a date, the 1st of July 2001 would see the transition. On returning from the USA in February of 2001, Ken spoke to me and said. "I cannot do this anymore you have to take it, you have two weeks"!

Thankfully, by this time Trish was a part of the ministry. She was supported by Steve in helping me and so we took over the program.

A few weeks later, I met Dr Stan DeKoven, the president of the AMERICAN version of Vision – Vision International University. Stan has been a good friend and an encouragement as the colleges continued to grow.

Ken and Stan had been working to get Vision accredited and make accredited awards available throughout the Vision network. The process was costly and time consuming, it required the accreditation of every subject. Unknown to them, this plan was doomed to failure due to certain directives of the accrediting agency. I discovered a Christian

Ministry and Theology program being offered that we could purchase, we could use our Vision material to fulfil the study needs. Taking advantage of this option meant that we did not need to get each subject accredited.

The original Vision Christian College program was retained and it continues to this day. We appreciate the relationship we have with the USA that allows us to offer their State Approved degree program from the Bachelors Completion to the Ph.D.

Vision International College was born as a separate entity by using our existing study material. With some additional workload for each award level, we successfully gained full Recognised Training Organisation (RTO) status in 2003. We were the first bible college to offer the Christian Ministry and Theology courses. At that stage, we offered Cert III and IV, diploma and advanced Diploma; this has since been extended to the Graduate Certificate and Graduate Diploma.

To this date, we have been involved in offering this program to students and student bodies around the world, we assist other colleges in offering the courses as well. It is being established in Kenya, South Africa, as well as in Mauritius and Uruguay in South America. Other requests are coming is as well making it possible to run a Vocational bible college in developing nations. Students from Canada, the United States, the UK and Europe are working through the subjects to gain their awards without leaving their home or their ministry. We have over 1000 students that have enrolled in Vision International College since 2003, while some 3000 have enrolled in Vision Christian College and some 550 students enrolled in the Internet Bible College.

The internet Bible College is still the vehicle through which we are able to offer all of our courses http://www.internetbible college.com or http://www.visioncolleges.net. This continues to attract students to Vision Christian College, Vision International College, and Vision International University.

In Australia, Vision College now appeals to various denominations. Through our individual study programs and through our Local Church bible college programs known as Resource Centres, this has proven to be a valuable resource for the mission field. This allows them the option to set up colleges in the field.

In times of drought and recession, good times and plenty, we see a constant stream of students coming back. An often heard plea has been, "I did Vision 20 years ago... Can I do some more studies...?"

We have as students from young to middle aged to the elderly; laymen and pastors, missionaries and deacons, men and women from all walks of life have done, are doing and will continue to call on us, as we are able to meet the various needs of those seeking to study the word of God.

As to missions we have kept an eye on the needs overseas, taking Vision to Myanmar, Nepal, France, England and Scotland, India, Vietnam, Papua New Guinea, Fiji, the Philippines, Mauritius, South Africa, Zimbabwe, China and we are currently looking to Pakistan.

Our oldest student is a 93-year-old pastor who contacted me by phone from the USA and said. "I am a pastor and I have been in ministry for 60 odd years, I think it time I did some serious study." I waived his fees... such an honour to minister to someone like that. Our youngest student is a 14-year-old youth who is determined to study and be something for God.

As mentioned earlier this is not the work of an individual but a team of people who have learned and are skilled in extraordinary ways to meet the needs of the college.

Firstly, to honour both Ken and Alison who have been a great strength in times of need and helped to walk us through some very difficult times.

Steve and Trish Hart; Trish joined us a year after starting the Internet Bible College, Steve decided to join us a few years later following his heart attack. Elaine Ryan, who passed away a few years ago, joined us and was an incredible strength to us in the early days of VIC, Jane Ryan joined us recently as a volunteer, and my wife Rosalind who is more of a silent partner, but without her strength and life, I could not hope to fulfil this ministry

Steven Hart – In charge of Production at Vision College, Minto, New South Wales

I am Trish's husband (Trish is the registrar at Vision) and we work together at the Vision Head office in Minto, New South Wales. We have been together for 34 years now and have 3 sons, 1 daughter and 4 grandsons. I began working for Vision after a heart attack, which meant I could no longer do any heavy work and needed to take on a lighter task. Over the years that I have worked for Vision, I have grown in many new and interesting directions, learning everything I needed to get the work done.

I work constantly in the background, doing all those extra tasks that many like to avoid, the things that seem unimportant. Instead, I find those things are extremely necessary to the smooth running of the office. They are the kinds of things that would irritate most people, but are exactly what I enjoy.

When our children were younger, we used to take them abseiling (rappelling), and my wife Trish would take the lead into the caves. I would bring up the rear, making sure that everyone got through the cave, up the ladder, and down the side of the mountain. Working at the Vision office and in our Church, I do the same sort of thing. I am often planning well in advance, and then staying behind to keep things in running order.

Some of the specific tasks I do are presentation, preparation, and planning for seminars; searching for great book covers for Ken and Alison's books, printing books, storing things and doing any other task I see that needs to be done. I would call myself a good support person most of the time.

I enjoy my job at Vision very much, but like all things, it has its moments. As we all know, life is not without its problems.

Patricia Hart – Registrar of Vision College, Sydney, Australia

I am Steven's wife, and I can tell you that he is a great man. He is kind, longsuffering, patient, slow to anger, did I mention patient? Yes, all of these qualities are in him, and I greatly appreciate that he has been able to stand with me through the joys, demands and rigours of our life together. He is the best friend I have ever had, truly the best! I'm also a mother and Grandma, as Steven has related above.

How did you first get involved with Vision? In 1994 I began studying with Vision College and half way through, I had a strange thought, that one day, I could run Vision Colleges, which I shared with Ps Michael York, (I believe he laughed at the time). It was quite absurd ... to have that thought, as I was busy working 2 jobs, throughout the day, and studying at TAFE College in business and administration and accounting at night school, as well as raising our young family. Besides that, the fact that both Ken and Alison were still running the Colleges meant it was just a thought which was put on the shelf, and left to collect dust (so, to speak)

(I believe that Ps Michael York thought I would not be the ideal candidate for this role!) And to be honest, back in the state, that I was in, at that time, it would have appeared ludicrous to him, and if others knew, they may have said the same as well. But look what God can do, even though, it appeared that my life was going nowhere, just an ordinary housewife, as some say, I ignored them all, and kept attending night school, even though there was no justifiable reason to do so at the time. It appeared to be a waste of money to many onlookers and advisors.

I completed Cert IV in bookkeeping and Cert III in administration and business. This enabled me to work through to Share Care and learn Not For Profit accounting principles and business practices, which ideally suits the church and the College. After some encouragement from Denis, to finish my studies, in 1996, I finally completed my Diploma of Theology studies.

1996 – 2000 I worked as a volunteer in the College 2-3 days a week, while earning an income from another part time job at Share Care Inc, a disability organisation. This was a transitional learning curve preparing me for the diverse workloads at Vision Colleges Inc.

In 2000, Steven survived a massive heart attack, leaving him with only half his heart working. This led us to devote all of our time in the Colleges as volunteers, allowing me to serve in many varied roles, as Secretary, Treasurer, Registrar, and one of the Director's.

After completing the recognised study course, I enrolled in the accredited course and completed

Cert IV 2005
Diploma 2010
Advanced Dip 2011
Grad Cert April 2012

Currently enrolled Graduate Diploma, which I aim to complete before the end of this year (God willing).

You cannot imagine how much these studies have changed everything, the information inside each book, is like reading about a family of people. I embraced it all; education, literature, the arts, travel, the word, even though it includes the struggles of life, it shows how they managed to effectively place themselves under Gods protection. At the same time, it has effectively released others, just like myself, allowing us to press into the blessings and promises of God.

How much do I enjoy the work I do at Vision? I wanted to be involved in evangelism. When you think about it, what better way than to be here, offering training to the saints so they can get on with their work? I get involved in almost everything in regards to the day-to-day activities of the Colleges.

My gifting is in administration, and I operate in this area with ease. Accounts, debtors and creditors, all the finances; in addition I offer student support, and support to Ps Denis.

The most wonderful development for me has been the traineeship funding for our Certificate IV program, making it a viable new study pathway. It has been quite remarkable to watch God's hand of favour on this new avenue of study.

Our volunteers are a great help to us here at Minto. We could not manage without their help. First, we had David Castle – a retired man with many years of life experience in retail, he is married to Ruth, and they have four children. He came to Vision for one year, in 2011 -2012, and helped with the data entry needed for Accreditation.

Next, we have Jane Ryan. She is a retired, white, South African single lady. Jane comes in twice a week to enter student records and to do any other clerical duties that are needed. She is a delight to work with, and she has overcome many health obstacles.

A Graduation Speech Given In Sydney Australia
(Pastor David Holt, January 2009)

Mr. Presidents, Board of Directors, Fellow graduates, family and friends. May I begin by saying that I feel quite out of place being up here giving this speech on behalf of the student body. I have been honoured to be asked to deliver this speech but at the same time humbled to have been chosen.

My study experience with VCC began in very different circumstances. It began way back on the 29th January 1995, when after showing some initial interest in commencing study; I was sent a hand written note from Dr. Alison Chant. She advised me that as she had heard of some personal difficulties I was undergoing and because I had shown some interest in studying with Vision, that she had decided to send me three units to commence my studies to assist me through what turned out to be some very turbulent times. I thank Dr. Alison for those initial units because that really did commence my hunger to learn.

My hunger to learn was not in order to receive awards, certificates or degrees, but rather to learn and understand God more in my life. Sure the awards etc. were great motivations and I appreciated them along my journey of study, but my main premise for study has and will always be, to understand God, his word, and my part in his family more. With that in mind, my encouragement to anyone who asks me about studying the Bible is to study for the purpose of learning, as it's not all about awards and certificates. Awards are great and will definitely come but always make the priority learning more about God.

With that in mind, I think it is such a privilege to study God and his Word. As all of you here today who are receiving awards can testify, the study of the Bible and God, although awesome, is not easy. We all come here with our own personal beliefs, understandings and pre-conceived ideas of the word of God only for them then to be ripped apart and refashioned into something more like the way God wants us to think.

I remember reading a book many years ago by a man named Jerry Cook and it was titled "Everything I have Learned Since I Knew It All". Now I am not saying that I entered into this field of study knowing it all, in fact far from it, but just when you think you may know something, that you're beginning to get an understanding on a certain subject, you are then forced to rethink, re-access and examine what it is you thought you knew.

Then, when you think you have a good NEW understanding on that same subject, you are then forced to go through that same process again. The study of the word of God is unlike any other form of study because we can never know it all. Our understandings and beliefs are constantly being challenged, re-evaluated and re-addressed as we come to have a greater knowledge of God and his word.

Our study of the word of God should never really stop, it should be the one constant thing we do in our life. We need to continue to pursue our study of the word of God, it is vital to our continued spiritual health and well-being. As the Apostle Paul said to Timothy:

"All scripture is God-breathed and is useful for teaching, rebuking, correcting and training in righteousness, so that the man of God may be thoroughly equipped for every good work".

Let us not see this achievement today as the end of our study, but allow it to be just another stepping stone to continue to learn and study all that we can regarding God and his word, that we may be thoroughly equipped for every good work that he may call us to do.

We have a great opportunity to study a book that is unlike any other book known to man. This book is alive, it's relevant and has been authorised by the creator of all things, God! There have been some great books written throughout history, but this book is second to none. You could read this book for 100 years and still be getting some fresh revelation from it in year 101. In the words of the book of Hebrews:

"For the word of God is living and active. Sharper than any double edged word, it penetrates even to dividing soul and spirit, joints and marrow; it judges the thoughts and attitudes of the heart."

What an awesome privilege it is to study such a magnificent book, a book that is LIVING and ACTIVE. Fellow graduates, my encouragement to you today is to keep up your studies and learn all you can about our awesome God!

With all that in mind, I would like to say thank you to the example that has already been shown to us in regard to this continual study and the encouragement of improving ourselves in God and his word. To those men and women that challenge us with every new unit of study.

These dedicated people show us what it is to continue to want to know God better. They have dedicated their lives to study, having trodden the path well before us, and today they dedicate themselves to helping us achieve those same goals.

I speak of Dr's. Stan DeKoven, Ken and Alison Chant and Denis Plant. There are others also but most of our studies come from these learned people. We all value their study and commitment to bring God's word to people like you and me. Without these amazing people, we would be poorer in our knowledge of God, poorer in our spiritual health and well-being.

Today I would like to thank each and every one of you for your uncompromising search for the truth of God and your everlasting input into mine and my fellow graduates lives.

On a personal note, I would like to especially thank Dr. Ken and Alison Chant for always making yourselves available to me whenever I had the urge to phone or tap your brains at conferences. Thank you, you have assisted me in unspeakable ways and I would not be standing up here today if it was not for your encouragement along the way. Thank you so very much.

To our families, wives, husbands, mothers, fathers, brothers, sisters, and children who have taken this journey with us and have sacrificed along the way. Without your love and support we would not be here today, we all thank you.

To the staff at VCC, whose dedication to make our study life much easier is unparalleled? Particularly people like Patricia Hart, to whom I have made numerous phone calls asking probably the most unusual and definitely un-profound questions ever, but who is always so obliging, loving and patient. VCC is a brilliant place to learn with some of the best theological minds around and a staff that shows the true nature and heart of God. Why would anybody study anywhere else but VCC? Thank you to all at Vision!

Finally, to all my fellow graduates today, no matter what award, certificate or degree you have achieved in this past year, let us look forward to what God will teach us in 2009 and beyond as we continue to diligently study his word with even more vigour and excitement than ever before. There is so much yet to learn, with so little time to learn it in. Keep up your learning so that we may all be thoroughly equipped for every good work that our Lord and Master may call us to do. Let us use our time wisely, making sure we give quality time to learning more about God and his word in 2009 and beyond.

Congratulations to every one of you and may God richly bless your continued study and life with him. God bless you all!

Chapter Thirteen

The Conception and Development of Vision in the USA

This is the story of the men of God who have come alongside us to spread the Whole Word to the Whole World. Following the wonderful plan of God, at the same time as we were establishing our correspondence courses in Australia, other dedicated men of God were following a similar path in the USA.

The following two interviews were given to explain the beginnings of the Vision History USA in preparation for the 40th Anniversary of Vision in 2014.

They will explain how Vision was conceived and developed from the perspective of Dr. Stan DeKoven and Bishop Randy Gurley who had a remarkably similar vision to Ken Chant of Australia. God in his wisdom brought the three men together during the time Ken and Alison were living in the USA.

Dr. Stan Dekoven – California, USA

Dr Stan has an interesting background, which has provided him with unique skills in communication and has given him remarkable insight into the hearts of men and the workings of churches and institutions. He is able to go into a country and find a man who is trustworthy, with a deep desire to spread the Word of God and teach the deep things of God. Because of this, he has been one of the reasons Vision has spread now to so many countries. His willingness to stay on track, travelling constantly to support and encourage the men and women he has discovered, has been one of the reasons why Vision is still growing and developing so wonderfully.

Stan was born and raised in San Diego, CA, the middle child of three, but eldest son, to Ron and Louise DeKoven. Their family home was the center of activity, as they had very little in the way of material things, but the children weren't aware of their poverty until they reached high school age. Their home was filled with love and anger, hurt and family solidarity...a mass of dysfunction, as Stan has alluded to in many of his books. His sister is 3 ½ years older, and his brother is 2 ½ years younger, all three are products of a small local church and public school.

Early in the life of the children, Ron and Louise, who wanted private time together on Sunday mornings, would send them to the local Sunday school. This was a time of learning, love and fun. Fortunately, the local church was a Bible believing one (Evangelical Methodist) as it could have been a cult and Stan's parents would not have known the difference. In 1963, prompted by the assassination of President John F. Kennedy, Louise decided she would go to church. She had always believed in God, but not in the church as such. She realized, with Camelot falling down, she needed God and so before the Pastor could complete his sermon she was at the front of the church demanding him to lead her to Christ. She insisted the whole family go to church and, in early February 1965, at 12 years of age, at that same little church, Stan gave his heart to the Lord. Over time his two siblings joined him in his faith, and last of all Ron. After much nagging and encouragement from Louise, Ron gave his heart to the Lord.

In August of that same year, at a church camp with a missionary speaker, Stan sensed God's definite call on his life. His focus for the next 5 years was to be in church as much as possible, serving, witnessing, praying, preaching whenever he was given a chance (his pastor, Lee Speakman believed in training his converts in the local church). In this atmosphere, Stan grew fairly strong in the Lord, in spite of difficulties within and without.

In 1970, Stan met Dr. Joseph Bohac, who became his second pastor and lifelong friend and coworker. This was during the Jesus People days, and Stan discovered that Doc, who was his High School English teacher, was a Pentecostal, tongues talker, which he thought was very interesting. They discussed the Baptism in the Holy Spirit together, and Stan was encouraged to seek the experience. He received the Baptism at a local church in the Southern part of San Diego, one that sadly became quite cultish, but God was gracious. Stan was given a word from the Lord to go, to receive, and never return to that church. Fortunately, he was obedient to that word from God so he was not caught up in the cult that formed there. Because of his baptism, Stan experienced a genuine presence of the Lord in a deeper way than ever before, and due to his naiveté, he came back to his church and "demonstrated" tongues for the youth group. Due to the rigidity of the Evangelical Methodist Church at that time, he was given the left foot of fellowship. He did not leave on the best of terms, but later returned and apologized for his wrong attitude towards his precious pastor, Lee Speakman.

Upon completing high school, Stan went to San Diego State University on a baseball scholarship, playing varsity baseball for two years, meeting and marrying his sweetheart Karen, and graduating in 3 years with a bachelor's degree in psychology, a thoroughly useless degree he felt. He then went on to graduate school, entered the US Army, and completed his Master's degree. During this time, Stan and Karen had two beautiful daughters' who have become long term workers for Vision. Rebecca (Volosin) has a daughter, Kaitlyn, and Rachel (Romero) has a daughter Daniela and son Adrian. Stan has always gained much happiness from his family.

Upon his return from the Army, which he found a tough experience, he completed his Ph.D. for the Professional School of Psychological Studies and later completed theological studies (Master of Divinity and a Doctor of Ministry from the Logos Graduate School and the Evangelical Theological Seminary respectively.

On completing his degrees, Stan started a counseling practice with a former partner, and it was quite successful financially, with offices around the county. This was a good time for Stan, but deep down he felt he was not keeping to his original call from God to preach and teach. Instead, he was succeeding as a Christian business man. He knew there was nothing wrong with being a professional counselor, but God had called him to a different life task. During that time, he met some key people who helped to shape the next 25 years: Dr. David Mendez, Evangelist Al Furey, and Dr. Ken Chant.

Dr. Mendez was the purported founder of Logos Bible College, aka Logos Theological Seminary, aka Logos Christian College and Graduate School. Quite by chance and in keeping with providence, Stan had been looking for an educational institution or program that would give him the opportunity to preach or at least teach. He saw a small ad in *Charisma* magazine about a school called Logos and decided to call to harass them in fun, as the counseling ministry he was in partnership with, though it was called Pelican Family Institute, was a program of the local Logos Foundation, which had been started by Dr. Bohac.

Stan tried calling the, at this time they were headquartered in Fort Worth, Texas, but they had had many varied addresses over the years, so it took much trouble and searching to find them. Finally, Stan was able to talk to Dr. Mendez who happened to be in the office when Stan phoned. Stan found Dr Mendez friendly and truly engaging, and they became great friends. Over time, Stan began to do some teaching for Logos, and quickly became the graduate dean, then the vice-president, with a promise to be president. Sadly, Stan discovered later that this position had been offered to many others as well. Eventually the whole operation moved into Stan's offices, then into the Grace Christian Fellowship Church offices where Dr. Ken and Alison were reluctantly pastoring.

About this time, Stan met Al Furey who was looking for a church to pastor and wanting to settle his family after many years of traveling evangelism. Stan was the worship leader and Karen and he were leading the Children's ministry in a church where Stan was recognized as co-Pastor. Al originally came to their church to conduct a crusade, but soon learned that the senior pastor at the time was longing to return to Canada, and soon did so. Al was then voted in as Pastor based on his remarkable evangelical and preaching gifts. Stan learned much about ministry from Al, though the trial he went through at this time was immense. The church finally decided to merge with Grace Christian Fellowship. Sadly this merged church finally disintegrated, though not before Stan learned some very valuable lessons that were to stand him in good stead in later years. Amid this sad time of learning, Stan was to meet Ken, and that was a divine encounter. They met through Stan's counseling ministry.

At this time Stan was Associate pastor, teaching part time for Logos, and still carrying a full counseling load. Originally, Dr. Chant had been asked to run a Bible School for Grace Christian Fellowship. Soon however, he ended up trying to pastor a rag tag band of believers. This was the result of poor management and problems with the former pastor. Many of the believers were so wounded they ended up in Stan's counseling office. Stan decided that he should meet this Australian who was pastoring Grace Christian Fellowship, so he set up a lunch appointment at Tio Leo's restaurant in San Diego, near the church. They met and became instant friends. Ken shared his vision for Bible education, and Stan shared his passion of practical teaching in the local church.

Sadly, they were only able to work together for a short time. This was a most difficult time for both of them for soon the Logos program blew apart, as a result of the problems with leadership. Stan nearly gave all of Ken's books to Logos, which would have been disastrous. Fortunately, Stan was given the rights to the books and soon began to write his own, using what he learned from his education, both at the University and from his life of helping and counseling.

Stan and Dr. Gurley, whose story follows, felt that the curriculum Ken had written was a breath of fresh air. It was a conservative charismatic curriculum, based upon Biblical theology, and added to Stan's own focus on practical theology, it seemed to blend well. Stan became thoroughly convinced that the blending of the two, along with the work of many other authors who have been added to the Vision curriculum, is a continued blessing to our English language students. Now it also blesses students in multiple languages around the world.

The original curriculum was designed for complete correspondence studies, and mainly for pastors who had never had opportunity to properly study before assuming their responsibilities. Part of Stan's contribution to the Vision Program was what he had learned with Dr Mendez and his friend and partner Dr. Gurley. This was the importance of Church based training-- that is, using the local church and its programs of worship and service, along with local instructors, mainly the pastors themselves, as a major part of the program. The textbooks, study guides and exams make up the core of the academic program, but additional inspiration and accountability for service comes through the life of the church. Packaging this for local churches was Stan's focus, and this Resource Center emphasis has now stretched globally, to nearly 150 nations of the world.

During the process of moving from Logos to Vision and setting up the church based program, Karen, Stan's wife was a pillar of strength. Stan pays tribute to her and others of his staff in San Diego.

He says, *The truth is that without my strong and mostly quiet partner, Karen, who wholeheartedly supported our pursuit of Logos and then Vision, which put at risk our very comfortable life style, I could not have accomplished what I have. I am most grateful to Karen, who was our primary in house administrator of Logos/Vision from 1989 until her diagnosis with brain cancer in 1998... I miss her every day. I honor also my hard working team. My daughters and son-in-law Danny Romero and all of our supporting staff throughout the years--Tal, Dee, Delores, Kelly and many others who have helped bring Vision to the place it enjoys today.*

Probably the most frustrating part of the program for Stan has been the difficulty in achieving US accreditation. This has increasingly become a need for students wanting to do market place service rather than pastoral ministry. Even more than the current recession, the lack of accreditation weighs on Stan's heart. He believes sincerely that it would strongly enhance both the marketability and acceptability of Vision awards, even though he is completely convinced that our curriculum and delivery systems can rival any in the world. Vision would be greatly helped if it had accreditation. However, we do have our present State Approved status and our vocational accreditation in the great land of Australia.

For over twenty years, Stan has travelled for Vision to over 85 nations of the world. Everywhere he goes he is loved and accepted. He has a unique ability to make everyone feel at home with him. This has stood him in good stead in places like Ireland, the incredible mission fields of Kazakhstan, Ukraine and Kuwait, the continents of Africa, and Australia. He loves to see vibrant Christianity up close and personal, but his favorite place remains in Ramona, with his daughters and their families.

His special joy is working with Drs. Randy and Manon Gurley. They have worked together for over 25 years. He also takes joy in being a co laborer with great men and women of God such as Dr. Tim and Laurie Dailey, Dr. Steve and Kathy Mills, Dr. Gail Stathis and Dr. Brian van Deventer, Dr. Ron Bernier, Dr. Kim Sam Seong and family. Dr. Eugene Smith now in Ireland, Dr. John and Iris Delgado, Dr. John and Hepsi Ezekiel, and of course our Vision family in Australia with Drs. Ken and Alison, and Dr. Denis and Ros. He feels greatly blessed to work with these truly committed servants of God, around the world.

Stan feels the translation of the books into various languages has been a real struggle at times. *If Vision had sufficient money, we would just hire folks and get it done", he says, "but we have partnered with our World Zone leaders in Russia, China, Latin America, etc., who have taken on the task as a part of their mission to do this vital work. It is slower, but the nations are taking ownership of the work, which is important for the long haul. Anyone who has some interest in terms of investing time and money into this project of translating the books will be the best ambassadors of the teaching and training programs we offer in those languages.*

"We have been blessed to partner with church planting ministries like Pastor Larry Stockstill's Surge ministry, which shares several of our World Zone leaders with theirs. Our trained students become the primary church planters, and with the work of Kim Sam Seong, Tim Dailey, Steve Mills and others. Vision is a part of facilitating the planting of hundreds of churches, around the world, for the glory of God, and the expansion of God's kingdom, the fruit of a vision started by God from Tasmania and San Diego in taking the Whole Word to the Whole World. Well, the best is yet to come."

Bishop Randolph Gurley – Maryland, USA

Bishop Gurley is Vision Director of World Missions. Here he writes of his call to the ministry and his involvement in the beginnings of Vision in the USA.

Bishop Gurley comes from a distinguished background. He has an honorable line of forebears who have been in Christian ministry for twenty-three generations. Men like Dr. Phineas Gurley who, as Abraham Lincoln's pastor and friend assisted the President in drafting the Proclamation of Emancipation document, and this Declaration is framed and hangs on a wall of the Presbyterian church Dr. Phineas Gurley pastored. Another distinguished ancestor, Rev. Randolph Gurley, attended the first abolition meeting in New York City and was co-founder of the African nation of Liberia.

Bishop Randolph Gurley was born again at the age of thirty. While on a short-term missions' trip with Nora Lam to Taipei, Republic of China, Japan, Korea and the Philippines he received the call from God to fulltime ministry. He entered South-eastern University in Lakeland, Florida, his hometown, in 1978. Since that time he has preached, taught, and held crusades and revivals all over the U. S. and around the world. He has authored three books: *Light not White* (Racism and the Church), *My Brother's Keeper* (A Study on World Evangelisation), and *The Ninth Man* (A fictional account of one of the Ten Lepers).

He was consecrated to the office of Bishop in 2004 and is President and Overseer of Harvest International Ministerial Fellowship of over 2,500 pastors worldwide. This year, 2008, marks 30 years of ministry for Bishop Gurley.

Today, 17th February 2008, Bishop Gurley and his wife, Dr. Manon Gurley, have just returned from a sweep through India, Cambodia, and Vietnam, where they have been preaching, teaching and, establishing Vision classes. They graciously agreed to describe his conversion, his accomplishments, and the early days of the Bible Schools which Dr. Gurley, as he was then, helped to establish from '83-'89 before the affiliation with Vision which came about in 1990.

How did it all begin? Gerald Kaufmann and Luciano Padilla and other inner city pastors in New York City became tired of sending their best young men and women away to Bible School only to find that they either did not return at all. If they did return, they found they had lost touch with the vision of the church and the people of the inner city.

For this reason, the pastors decided to set up classes in 1983 in urban and inner city schools. The idea was to keep the Bible students in their own church while they studied and so keep the local vision alive in their hearts.

This was a remarkably similar vision to the one given Dr. Ken and Alison Chant in Australia in 1974 as their church too had lost young people to a Bible College, who did not then return after graduating. They determined to help other pastors in a similar position to train their own people and so Dr. Chant began writing the necessary curriculum.

About this time, the Logos Bible College moved its head office to California where Dr. DeKoven had a successful Family Counseling Center and Dr. DeKoven began developing the graduate program for the college.

When the original Logos Bible School President, David Mendez, resigned in 1987, he offered the position to Dr. Gurley who, because he was travelling as a minister, nationally and internationally, and because he did not want to relocate to California, where the head office was now situated, in turn offered the Presidency to Dr. Stan DeKoven. Dr. DeKoven was already living in Ramona, California and was able, with his wife Karen, to set up and maintain an office to handle the students. Dr. Gurley then took the position of Vice President.

Now that Dr. DeKoven and Dr. Gurley were President and Vice President of Logos Bible College, they continued opening campuses across the US and around the world. During this time, Dr. Gurley also opened the first campuses in Nigeria, India, and Puerto Rico.

In 1990 just before Dr. Ken and Alison Chant moved back to Australia, Dr. Gurley, Dr. DeKoven and Dr. Chant met in California and Dr. Gurley and Dr. DeKoven decided to officially join with Dr. Chant in his Vision Bible College and to change the name of Logos Bible College to Vision Bible College. Part of the reason for this merger was because Dr Chant had a similar vision and a strong original curriculum through the books he had written. These added to the Logos curriculum would make Vision unique in that it would be suited to third world countries as well as to the first world. Now the two Bible Colleges have grown and developed into what is known as Vision International University.

Dr. Gurley called all the campuses that were working with the original college, and 80% of these campuses were happy to move with Dr. Gurley and Dr. DeKoven into Vision. "Where *you go we go*" was their general decision.

From that time on Dr. Gurley looked after the campuses on the east of the Mississippi River and Dr. DeKoven looked after those on the west of the river. At this time Dr. DeKoven also had the help of Dr. Bohac, who has since gone to be with the Lord.

Later Bishop Gerald Kaufmann stepped down from being chairman of the Board of Regents and Dr. Gurley took his place and he still holds that position.

Dr. Gurley (now Bishop) since 2004 also holds the position of Director of World Missions for Vision and that explains why he and Dr. Manon have just completed their latest Missions tour, mentioned in this article.

As with many of the Vision staff, the Gurley's, as well as their work for Vision, double as pastors of a wonderful church in Baltimore, which willingly undergirds the missions work. It is wonderful that so many men and women, like the Gurley's, have linked together to help take the Chant's original vision "The Whole Word to the Whole World" into 153 countries and 7,000 churches so far. The student body now covers over 100,000 students who are all learning the Word of God and studying theology.

Those students who have graduated are beginning to plant churches. So far, 5,000 churches have been planted in partnership with the Global 12 Project under Dr. Steve Mills, who is another of the marvellous team of Vision dedicated to the teaching and training of as many Christians as possible for the purpose of evangelism and the planting of more churches in the third world.

Brian Deventer - Greece

Brian Deventer was born in Rapid City, South Dakota, USA, the grandson of a pioneer church planter in the northern Midwest of the country. He is the son of a pastor and the nephew in a family full of ministers. His mother's family were farmers in North Dakota who ministered in their churches on the weekends. So ministry runs deep in his family.

Brian was educated in a denominational Liberal Arts college, doubling his studies in business administration and ministry. Athletics were the real passion of his life through high school and college, but that was taken from him through multiple injuries.

Upon graduation, he moved to Greece to assist some friends with a new church plant. The commitment was for three months. He has been there now for twenty years. During this time, outreach into the Middle East and North Africa, along with parts of Southeast Europe, became a driving force for Brian and has kept him on the "foreign mission field" for all this time.

Like many church kids, Brian came to the Lord early in life. He made his first commitment to the Lord at the age of nine in the church his father pastored in Vancouver, BC, Canada. The guest ministers happened to be those that Brian would eventually come to serve in Greece. His teenage years took him away from any real concern for the Lord, not that he stopped believing, but more that he stopped caring. That remained true until sometime in the second half of his first year of college.

Brian ended up attending the denominational school of his church by default. He had intended to go to college through sports, but that hope was taken away from him because of his injuries. As his father was the Vice President of the college at that time, tuition costs were free to him. It was agreed he would attend this college for at least one year before moving on somewhere else. In that time, God found and convicted him once again. He made a commitment to the Lord he vowed would be lasting and he has walked with God ever since.

His hunger for God grew quickly. He started ministering on weekends in area churches and his summers were spent contributing his efforts to his home church while working. This hunger brought him eventually to seek more profound things. In a chapel service at his college, the Lord baptized him with His Spirit, changing the course of his life forever.

Brian had always wanted to be involved in business somehow. Yet his activities, interests and studies were leading him more and more toward full time Christian ministry. Through trial and error, starts and stops, he has found ways to integrate the two little by little. His call is to see this region of the world that he serves affected by the Kingdom of God by means of church development, educational training, and business development through members of the local church.

Brian's degrees are impressive. Bachelor of Science, Tomlinson College (USA) Master of Science, Imperial University College, (UK) Master of Leadership, Vision International University (USA) Doctor of Ministry, Vision International University (USA)

He was ordained in 1992 with the Church of God of Prophecy, in 1997 with Evangel Fellowship International and in 2011 with Covenant Life Ministries (all based in the USA).

He co-founded in 1996, and has helped to direct, European and Middle Eastern Ministries, Inc. He has served as the General Director since 1998, and this has been his primary service roll.

He also served as Associate Pastor of the Glyfada Christian Center in Greece from 1992 to 1995, as Lead pastor from 1995 to 2000, and again as Associate Pastor from 2000 until now.

As well as these ministries that Brian has been blessed to share in, he has had a hand in church planting and development in more than 12 countries over the years, and has been involved in mission more broadly in more than 30 countries

Brian first contacted Vision because he was searching for a way to assist teachers in the Mission's Christian School in Greece to get some level of education to advance the cause of the school. The Vision program, in cooperation with the Association of Christian Schools International, gave Brian and his co-workers an opportunity to grant diplomas and receive teacher certification. This, in early 2000, was their only interest at the time.

Gradually, as they became more involved with communication with Dr. DeKoven, their offices were asked to consider more active rolls with Vision. Step-by-step they took on more responsibility for helping schools in their regions (Mediterranean and Western Europe), until Brian became the Zone Leader for the Mediterranean while Gail Stathis, his co-worker in Greece, became Zone Leader for Western Europe. They then began to develop small amounts of curriculum and to share in the broader vision of Vision International University.

Brian appreciates the Bible-centeredness and practical approach of much of the Vision curriculum, because the passion to see local churches become all that they can be shines through it. The flexibility of the system is very helpful, but the strength of Vision, sometimes not realized or synergized, is in the people and relationships that are enjoyed by all who participate.

Vision is also helpful in training lay persons in local churches, for ministerial training for those entering the ministry, and for training teachers in the Christian Education program. Most significantly, it is used for training leadership in many parts of the region – a growing exercise.

Vision allows development of a "Practitioner's Program" in the Master of Arts (both Leadership and Christian Education) that Brian has found most profoundly affecting. He has been involved in education of various sorts, venues and methods throughout the years, but this program has been the most fun, energetic and effective experience Brian has organized. It centers on those already involved in primary leadership in a "by invitation" experience that couples self-training with peer training, overseen by proctors and guest contributors. It has been fantastic for those involved to see primary leaders from across the region enjoy and grow through this experience.

Brian has explained that in Greece and the surrounding countries education is different and challenging, and not only for reasons of language and the scarcity of materials available. The traditional methods of lecture, reading, writing and test taking seem neither effective, nor too interesting. Brian and his co-workers have seen the growth of collaborative, interactive adult education grow. Vision allows credible ways to approach this, and they are excited especially for the opportunities for training leadership.

Brian has written two books *Beginning to Manage*, an introduction to basic management principles and *I Believe In*, a basic doctrines book based upon the Apostle's Creed.

Other Vision books are slowly being translated into Arabic as an ongoing program. The books are being translated slowly as they are implemented into programs within the region.

In Greece, two programs are operating in local churches, with an extension in Cyprus. There is a program operational in Lebanon, and one in Egypt. Other students are extension students operating through the regional offices. The program in Egypt has a nominal church planting program attached to it. The mission is currently seeking two new church plants in the next two years.

Vision Office Staff

Delores Horsman, MA – One of the Office Staff at Ramona California.

I started out as a volunteer helping to catalogue library books and posting grades to grade sheets. After five years of volunteering, I graduated to payroll. Now I work with online counseling students, grading their work and interacting with them. I also deal with international resource centers, processing their documents and issuing degree certificates. I often edit/proof read books for Vision Publishing. I am currently re-writing one of our counseling courses. I also oversee the International Association of Christian Counseling Professionals, our certifying agency for Christian Counselors, whether lay counselors or doctoral. I am working on upgrading the syllabus for our Masters Counseling program. There are some other projects on the list, but you get the idea.

I received my MA degree in Christian Counseling from Vision in 1998. I am currently working on my PhD. ("and miles to go before I sleep")

I was born and raised in Canada and immigrated to the USA with my parents when I was 14 years old. I have been married to my husband John for 44 years. We have two sons, Jeff, who lives locally, and Terry who lives with Jesus.

In the early 90's my husband and I were having relationship problems. Both of our sons were having their own difficulties. Terry had a friend who knew Dr. DeKoven and recommended Terry get some counseling from him. At the time, Dr. DeKoven was part of a conference in San Diego, so we went to see him and check him out. Terry ended up counseling with Dr. DeKoven regarding his struggles with homosexuality. Terry also found out during this time he was HIV positive. My husband and I ended up divorced. After a year, my husband gave his life to Christ and we did some counseling with Dr. DeKoven. John and I were re-married with Dr. DeKoven doing the service and our two boys standing with us. The wedding was in October. Come March of the next year Terry passed away and Dr. DeKoven did Terry's service for us.

In June (1994) Dr. DeKoven called me to see how I was doing and asked if I might be interested in doing some volunteer work for Vision. This seemed like a good idea and I also knew Dr. DeKoven wanted me to get out of my house and be more pro-active in the healing process. I have been here ever since.

I enjoy the work. The activities are varied so there is no room for boredom. It is a bonus working in a Christian environment. That does not mean things are perfect, but working for a Christian organisation is so much better than working 'out there'.

One of the things I have come to realize is that people are people wherever you go or live. We may have cultural differences. We may have different ways of dressing, cooking, worshipping, shopping, etc., but our hearts are all the same. We love and we want to be loved. As a woman, I see the hearts of women are the same wherever we live, regardless of our culture or environment. We share more things in common, than we have differences.

"Delores, sharing with you via email, it never ceases to amaze me how God picks and chooses his wounded soldiers who then become part of his strategy and prove such a blessing to others. God bless you for sharing so freely of your life and experiences"- Alison Chant

Ministries Who Work With Vision

Harold Eberle, President of Worldcast Ministries

Over the course of 18 years, we used Vision materials in our 12 Bible colleges, in seven countries of Africa. Now we have graduated over 6,000 students, of which approximately 1,000 are pastoring churches.

Today our work continues in the Middle East, where I oversee two pastor training schools, which are both using Vision materials. We have graduated about 100 students, but plan to train up several thousand throughout the Middle East.

Student Graduates

The following stories come from student graduates and teachers of Vision who are carrying on the good work in various countries around the world.

Alan Bullock - Student

For me personally, I elected to further my education by attending Vision International University and studying for a Master's in Counseling and a Doctorate in Ministry. Vision has helped me to grow and mature, not only in Biblical and counseling knowledge, but also in how to apply that knowledge with Godly wisdom, patience, love and faith in the pulpit and in my counseling ministry. Whether it is in the field of ministry, in a secular environment, in family situations, or in personal relationships, understanding Biblical truth and having faith in Jesus Christ and the power of love and prayer continues to pay many dividends, both in this world and certainly in the world to come for me as a student of Vision.

Karen Horsley – Graduate

My conversations with God were in a state of "murmuring and complaining" regarding the blatant rejection from a well-known Christian college due to their disagreement in the teachings of the church I was attending at that time.

During a visit with Dr. Anthony and Mary Spero, I relayed my story to Anthony who immediately called Dr. DeKoven; shortly after I was enrolled at Vision University. When I started, I had many past unresolved issues. Thank God, Dr. DeKoven was my mentor for those classes. Due to his insight, understanding, patience, and encouragement, all those issues were eventually resolved.

Vision is not just a University that trains and sends forth their students with head knowledge. Vision amplifies Jesus heart towards His children. Their teachings encompass the

WHOLE man, body, soul and spirit, and the healing of each. In the past 10 years, I have had 14 surgeries, 10 deaths, breast cancer and cancer on my face. Needless to say, I was NOT diligent in my studies, SHOULD have been expelled and would have by any other college. Vision kept encouraging me to complete the courses, which in doing so took my mind where it should have been. If Vision gave awards for the student who took the longest to graduate, I WOULD own that award!

Drs. Duane and Darilyn Bemis - Graduates

I am Dr. Duane Bemis and I graduated in 2007 from Vision International University, Ramona, CA with a Ph.D. in Christian Counseling. My wife, Darilyn V. Bemis has a BA in Theology 2012 from Vision International University of Florida, and this year she will graduate with her Masters Degree in Theology. My degree qualified me to be the Senior Chaplain over 3,500 inmates, 55 volunteers, one Assistant Chaplain, and four contracted chaplains in the Texas penal system.

Ten years ago, my wife and I started four churches at four prison facilities. We have approximately 20-inmates in leadership at each unit. At one unit, we started with one inmate who came each week. Now our monthly attendance at that one unit is over 2,000 men.

We started a two-year international discipleship program. Our inmates will be deported once they finish their sentence in the USA. I love to watch as the Lord transforms these men into mighty men of valor.

Here are some of the LORD's success stories:

1. **Jonathan P.** - is living and ministering in Bogotá, Columbia. He works for the University teaching English and has been on Christian Television sharing his testimony.

2. **Jose G.** - is living in Nuevo Laredo, Mexico and he works at his local church as their Secretary of Evangelism. He also oversees six home bible study groups. He is now married; he and his wife ministers together.

3. **Adrian M.** - is in Monterrey, Mexico. Recently he was asked to preach and share his testimony at his church of over 500 people. The church had him preach to their youth group and recently asked that he and his wife become their youth pastors. Three other churches in the area have invited him to preach in their churches. They have started a young couples Bible study at a Starbucks. The attendance has reached over 40 and God has now planted in their hearts to start a Christian coffee shop for more outreach. He and his wife are ministering in a youth offender detention center in their city. Recently he was promoted at the bank he works for, and they moved him and his family to Brazil.

4. **Alberto B.** - is living and ministering in Cabo San Lucas, Mexico. Alberto translated for me while in prison and he led worship for us. He is now helping with the church worship team. Recently he was asked to start a new church in a city about 20 miles away. He is now Pastor Alberto.

5. **Luis H.** - is in Piedras Negras, Mexico and he is now a student with Vision International University of Florida.

6. **Frank P.** - ministers in Lima, Peru. Frank has organized a singing group to go into the prisons and minister to the lost in his own country.

7. **Eliezzar G.** - is in Matamoras, Mexico helping build a drug rehabilitation center. He is working for a local church and helps with missionary groups from the

USA as the churches official interpreter. He has organized a team and they are ministering in the local youth prisons

8. **Francisco G.** - is in Mexico City, Mexico and has been on the radio including in Guadalajara. He has worked for the Billy Graham Ministries and they recorded a miracle healing through the prayer of this one time prisoner. His local church has sent him into the prisons in Mexico City.

9. **Joe W.** - is a former California inmate, now a child of God who lives in Yucaipa, California and heads the local churches missionary trips to Africa and Japan. He has married a Christian girl who was raised on the mission field. He has been on two trips to Africa and one to Japan.

10. **Stephen S.** - another former California inmate, now a child of the King of kings, and his wife live in Oregon. He and his wife April took their church youth group to Russia and Mexico in 2008. They have made two missionary trips into Mexico and Columbia. They are now being asked to be the youth leaders of their home church.

11. **Torero C.** - is ministering in Acapulco, Mexico and he is building a two-story drug rehabilitation center for drug addicts on his ranch. He was a famous bullfighter in Acapulco. He sold his bulls and is building the drug rehab center and he has been on missionary outreaches to Panama, Honduras, and other parts of Mexico. He sent us photos of himself helping his pastor baptize about 20 people in the Pacific Ocean.

12. **Eleno S.** - is in Juarez Mexico and working with his pastor to continue to build God's Bride.

13. **Fernando -** is a worship artist like me! He is in Mexico City serving in his local church. He is the current youth pastor at his church.

14. **Armando -** is near Monterrey Mexico ministering in his local church and he is doing urban outreach services with two other brothers from behind the razor wires of Big Spring, Texas.

15. **Carlos A. -** is in Columbia ministering in his local church. He and his wife are now the youth pastors at their church.

16. **Adame -** is in Mexico and he and his wife are ministering in the Mexican prisons. She emailed us to tell us that she sees how God changed her husband in prison and the grace she received she must now share with those in prison.

17. **Jose A. -** another missionary to Honduras.

18. **Jose V. -** is also in Monterrey, Mexico, and his local church has him on the radio and he was our worship leader in the Airpark church in Big Spring, Texas. He started tithing to the church he was going to be a part of before he was released from prison. His church has helped him record a CD of his music and the sales of those CD's are aiding in his ministry in Mexico!

19. **Eleazar G. -** is working in Monterrey, Mexico, and working and serving in his local church. He is about to be married to a local Christian girl. He is attending a University and his uncle is paying the tuition. He is now able to help his mother financially. He is employed by an International Bank, and he is now the executive of the bank.

20. **Sergio -** is in Mexico and is serving on the worship team as lead electric guitar. He is busy doing the work of the Lord. The church is sending him into

the local prisons. Manny helped disciple this one time convict.

21. **Gerardo V.** - is serving in a church of 3,000 and when he went home he led his mother to the Lord, and she was baptized with about 30 other people through his church. Manny helped disciple this one time former inmate also. He too is in Monterrey, Mexico. To God be the Glory!

22. **Clemente** - is the worship leader in his home church in Acapulco, Mexico and his pastor has taken him on crusades in other countries. He is releasing a new CD called, "Parting with Jesus"; and wants me to design the cover. Praise be to God who still changes lives for the better. They did a free Christian concert in Mexico, Costa Rica, Acapulco y Guadalajara and Puerto Rico.

23. **Antonio M.** - is living now in Matamoras, Mexico and ministering in his local church. They are using our articles to advance the Kingdom of God.

24. **Christian E.** - is in Nigeria and he is a pastor of a church in a large denomination near Lagos, Nigeria.

25. **Victor D.** - is in Mexico and he is working in a church that was waiting for him to come. He is their pastor and he is working on establishing this church with Christian literature to disciple his sheep. Currently he is using the material he obtained while under the leadership of our discipleship program.

26. **Carlos A.** - is ministering in El Salvador and using our literature to reach the lost in his city.

27. **Johnny E.** - who has taken our literature to the Bahamas.

My wife and I began a Resource Center of Vision International University of Florida in Big Spring, TX in 2008. We now have students in San Angelo, TX, Eagle Pass, TX and Piedras Negras, Mexico.

1. One Student is a Methodist Pastor in Mexico.

2. One Student is an Assemblies of God Pastor in Mexico.

3. One Student is a Pastor of a non-denominational church in Mexico.

4. A Missionary couple who Pastor a Church in Eagle Pass, TX but live across the border in Mexico.

5. Young man who has asylum in USA because he was a police officer/investigator in Mexico and the Cartel wanted him murdered.

6. Worship leaders, a married couple are both advancing their education

7. Dr. Bertha Rodriguez, who runs a nursing school in Mexico and is a lawyer, is now obtaining her Doctoral degree in Theology.

8. Recently we graduated a Pastor in Texas with her Bachelor & Master's in Theology.

9. Various other students who are advancing their Christian Education.

Because of all this the Lord has enlarged our territory and we are ministering more and more in Mexico.

We have also published four books:

1. *Twice Broken Once Healed*: in English and Spanish

2. *The Carpenter's Apprentice*: in English and Spanish

3. *Plague of Darkness*

4. *Death is a part of Life*

Visit our website to see more that The Lord is doing through His Ambassadors. **www.fggbemis.org**

Larry Hrovat, M.Div. - Graduate

I received my M.Div. from VIU in 1988. At the time, I had a demanding international ministry schedule, which mandated individualized attention. Dr. Stan DeKoven and his staff personalized degree requirements. I have cherished my M.Div. degree since 1988. As difficult as it was at times to complete my degree, with a growing family and tough schedule, it was definitely a decision that has paid benefits for the last 30 years.

Dr. DeKoven and his highly professional staff have your best in mind. They will personally initiate your degree requirements, allow you to complete your degree at a distance and commit to you, with the highest ethical and moral standards until completion. They will be committed to your ministry success.

Christy Hosefelder (Graduate)

After years of church attendance, I was ready for more in-depth and academic learning. Missionary friends in Africa told me about the long-distance M.Th. program from Vision. It seemed to fit my needs for flexibility to work around a full-time job and family responsibilities. It also gave me the great advantage of studying in my native language while living abroad. Having attended 3 universities as well as having done a correspondence course from a fourth and graduate studies in another humanities field, I can attest to the quality of the Vision curriculum. For the most part, standard texts reflecting various denominational back-grounds provided the core instruction. Term papers or projects in related areas of interest helped to synthesize and internalize the information.

What one gets out of a program depends on the effort put in. In my case, that was a lot both ways! The increased knowledge base gave me more confidence to teach and disciple in church and para-ministry settings. Having a ministry degree not only increased accountability in lifestyle and decision-making but also became a means to model personal and professional growth opportunities, especially for younger women and international students.

Durch ihr Studium konnte eine Entwicklung im Leben von Christy Hosefelder beobachtet werden. Ihr Auftreten und Weitergeben biblischer Inhalte ist von einer größeren Sicherheit und Deutlichkeit geprägt.

As Christy's pastor, I have been able to observe the development in her life as a result of her M.Th. studies. She is able to deliver and present Biblical truths with increased confidence and clarity.

Mary M. Kagondu (Graduate)

I am sorry for the delay. I got this message from David Cerar. My name is Mary M. Kagondu. I work as an office Manager in East Africa Office for Vision International Education Network here in Kenya.

I joined Vision International University in 2001, just as a student from a village. After 2 years, I had completely changed a lot due to the nourishment I got in Vision. I was picked as a Librarian, receptionist, instructor and distance student grader year after year respectively. I have completed up to Masters Level, and I am doing the PhD with Dr. Steven Mills as my mentor. I didn't know one day I would be the Office manager for VIEN. Vision has been a great help for many Church leaders here in Kenya. Also I am proud to be a product of VIU because since then (very new in Ministry), I learned so many things. I used to have very low self-esteem, but now I thank God I visit so many churches teaching and preaching the word of God.

Some of the Vision Students here in Kenya have been Policemen and women, who have portrayed a great picture in our country due to what they have learned. Recently one of our former students was shortlisted for the post of assistant inspector of police. I was so grateful with her; she had shown an upright character and Ethics in the Government. This portrayed a wonderful picture as a Vision International University Family in the Kenyan Government and has shown that we really produce People of Substance.

Others have been shortlisted in many other ministries in the Government including the Counseling Institutions. I will live to thank God for Vision in all days for the spirit of nourishment and building of characters in God's people and also the Church leaders. God bless Vision as you take the word to the whole world.

Yvette D'Souza - Teacher

This is the remarkable testimony of Yvette D' Souza and the way God has led her through the years.

I was born in 1955 in a middleclass Roman Catholic family of 6 (my parents, two sisters, one brother and me). I come from India. I completed my studies in the year 1978 and started working at a very young age as my father told me that if I wanted to take college education I should work to pay for the tuition fees, as he could not afford it. My father, mother and younger sister are now with the Lord. My brother and elder sister have settled in Canada with their families. My elder sister's husband serves as an Evangelist in the house of the Lord. I am a widow, my husband went to be with the Lord in 1989 at the age of 33 and I was 32 then.

Due to great financial difficulties, I came to Kuwait to work with Al Sane group – Apple computers in 1991 through an agent. I did not have many friends here, as after the tragic loss I had become a sort of a recluse. For 8 long years I did not go to church, it was just work and home mainly because I did not know how to travel by bus and most of my colleagues at the office had warned me that I should be careful as I was a young, single woman on my own.

But during this time, I read my Bible, said my prayers daily, and always told the Lord that I wanted to go to church. Then after 8 long years as usual I was waiting for my transport to get me to work. I happened to meet 2 Christian ladies from the same building as I lived as their timings had changed because of Ramadan. As we chatted, they were surprised that they had never seen me for all these years though we were living in the same building. As I got to know them better one of the ladies asked me to help her brother get a job as he was on a visit visa. I promised to try and by God's grace managed to get him a job with residence in one of our sister concerns.

Then they asked me what gift I would like in return for this favor and I told them to take me to church. They brought me to the National Evangelical Church – Karnataka Congregation. At first I was worried when I realized I had not come to a Roman Catholic Church, but slowly my fears subsided as I realized that I had come here also to worship Jesus. I continued going there for a few months, when my heart's desire was to want to know more of the Lord. So I learned to travel by bus and started attending the English Language Congregation (now TLC) service but I was not satisfied. Then I began to attend all the services. It was here that I had an encounter with the Lord. I was saved and later was water baptized in 2000.

About this time I was introduced to the Vision program that was being conducted by The Lighthouse Church at the National Evangelical Church in Kuwait. I joined Christian Education and from the time I have joined these classes there has been no end to my quest to get to know more and more of the Lord. I also felt a strong urge to impart God's love to others by sharing my knowledge and experiences and serving in any capacity that would bring Glory to God, so I started teaching the children and facilitating ISOM classes and joined several ministries.

I love the Lord, and my heart's desire is to know and serve Him better in every way with my whole heart forever. Indeed our God is a good God who takes care of the widows who have no one else to turn to. Praise be to God our Father, Jesus His son, and the Holy Spirit!!!

Kerala – Where Pastor David Jones ministered for the last years of his life.

Our contact for Vision in Kerala is a business man, Babu Manjuran. Babu has set up an office and has financially supported our Vision College there.

Kerala in Southern India has a rich Christian heritage. The main port of Kerala is Cochin and here King Solomon built a Synagogue in thanks for the timbers that he was able to collect to build the Temple of God mentioned in 1 Kings chapters 5- 8.

In New Testament times Thomas, one of Jesus disciples, spent time preaching the gospel in Kerala. There are Christians who can trace their heritage back to Thomas and the church he founded there. Tradition indicates that Thomas performed many miracles but he faced fierce opposition and was finally martyred in northern Kerala.

David Jones has taught Vision classes for many years here in Australia and he visited Kerala, India, seven times and taught groups of pastors for Vision there as well as holding other evangelical meetings. David told us that working through an interpreter causes the teaching sessions to move slowly and Christian ideas and concepts have to be worked through constantly during lectures.

The work David began continues to grow and more and more Indian pastors are holding classes both in English and in their own language.

During his last visit David spoke to 230 Hindu students in the English Language School through a group called Wake Up India Ministries who work in the schools. They have indicated they would like to network with us in India.

Vision is also in Andhra Pradesh where a Pastor Emmanuel looks after the Vision classes.

David has not been able to return to Kerala for the last 9 months but Pastor Richard Murray, another Vision graduate, has also travelled to Kerala doing some teaching and evangelism for us. We have also been invited to work with another group of churches throughout Southern India so the college is slowly expanding. Who knows what the future holds!

When I wrote these words for the Vision history book we could not know that the immediate future would be the sudden death of David Jones our much loved son in law. We miss you David, but we know God is in control and he will make a way for others to take up the burden of Vision in India. Ken and Alison Chant.

Greetings from Vision, India!

It was with a heavy heart that I read the lines of your letter and we are so sad to hear that David has only a few days to live and we will keep praying for him and God can still work miracles.

I will ask all the Vision people here in India to pray for him.

I am sure that the conference will not be the same without David and India Vision is much indebted to his passion and care and he will always be with us. Please share our thoughts with Sharon who must be having a hard time in her life.

I do believe that Richard Murray or someone else will come to India to help us and we will miss David who was so passionate of India.

I know how difficult this is for you and Ken! We will keep you in our prayers!

Regards, Babu Manjuran

Vision Publishing offers numerous books and courses. These may be ordered by going to the website at www.booksbyvision.com or by contacting the Vision Publishing office at 1-800-9-VISION.

www.ingramcontent.com/pod-product-compliance
Lightning Source LLC
Chambersburg PA
CBHW071759090426
42737CB00012B/1877